The Widow's MIGHT

A Legacy of Love and Hope Rising

Maria Jasinskas, M.D.

WESTBOW
PRESS®
A DIVISION OF THOMAS NELSON
& ZONDERVAN

This book is a work of non-fiction. Unless otherwise noted, the author and the publisher make no explicit guarantees as to the accuracy of the information contained in this book and in some cases, names of people and places have been altered to protect their privacy.

Scripture taken from the King James Version of the Bible.

WestBow Press books may be ordered through booksellers or by contacting:

WestBow Press
A Division of Thomas Nelson & Zondervan
1663 Liberty Drive
Bloomington, IN 47403
www.westbowpress.com
1 (866) 928-1240

Because of the dynamic nature of the Internet, any web addresses or links contained in this book may have changed since publication and may no longer be valid. The views expressed in this work are solely those of the author and do not necessarily reflect the views of the publisher, and the publisher hereby disclaims any responsibility for them.

Any people depicted in stock imagery provided by Thinkstock are models, and such images are being used for illustrative purposes only.
Certain stock imagery © Thinkstock.

ISBN: 978-1-5127-3720-2 (sc)
ISBN: 978-1-5127-3722-6 (hc)
ISBN: 978-1-5127-3721-9 (e)

Library of Congress Control Number: 2016905413

Print information available on the last page.

WestBow Press rev. date: 04/05/2016

Contents

Foreword

I am a medical doctor who is a trained expert specifically in the field of psychiatry, and I wrote this book. Unlike a psychologist, I completed medical school and can prescribe medications. I have a license to practice in my state but need to make sure that you, the reader, understand the contents in this book should in no way be transferred as recommendations for treatment of your own suffering or loss. If you are dealing with thoughts of suicide, please get help for yourself. Do not make excuses to justify or rationalize taking your own life. The book is written to shed light on the unfortunate topic of suicide and in this case in particular, the suicide of my husband. This book is not written from the perspective of research findings or any other areas of medical expertise. The writing that follows is a compilation from my own direct personal experience. As difficult a topic as it is to discuss, suicide is unfortunately quite prevalent in today's society. My hope is that in disclosing my story, you will feel empowered by the knowledge gained and help me spread the word so that future generations will see suicide as a thing of the past. My husband was a strong person, a war-decorated veteran, and an exemplary citizen of society who served his country with honor and courage. Even with all the training I achieved in the area of psychiatry, the study of behavior and the brain, I never saw the signs of suicide I was trained to look for. In retrospect, after speaking with so many of my husband's friends, coworkers, and comrades, neither did they.

Once again, I reiterate that this book in no way should substitute for your own personal need to obtain help. If you are having thoughts of suicide, please do not make the choice my husband made. He died so you did not have to. Get help, please.

Also, in reading this book, I feel the need to caution you. I am an avid follower of Jesus Christ. I do hope you can push past whatever discriminatory thoughts you may harbor and just read the book to see what you can gather from it. My spiritual belief is not one of condemnation but of grace. My journey in life has led me to seemingly insurmountable challenges from which I have emerged victorious simply because of my faith in my God and the precious blood of His Son. I challenge you to avoid the urge to put the book down because of my frequent and pervasive mention of my God. I was born here in the United States of America as a first-generation Mexican-American migrant farmworker. My story is proof that America is still the land of the free *because of* the brave. I do not take for granted the blood spilled by all who have fought for the rights and privileges I am able to access as an American. I am honored and appreciative for your time and attention and pray for you to receive wisdom, revelation, and restoration as you spend this time reading my book. Lastly, in the name of my personal Lord and Savior, Jesus, I break any strongholds of depression or suicide that you may be battling.

Acknowledgments

Chambers, Oswald. *My Utmost for the Highest*

Holy Bible, King James Version

Kenik, David. *Armed Response: A Comprehensive Guide to Using Firearms for Self Defense.* Merril Press, 2005

PAWSTrainingGroup.com

TogetherWeServed.com

Troy Industries: Worldoftroy.com

Introduction

This book is written for those of us who have personally had to endure major loss. It is my hope that in reading this book of tragedies and triumphs, you can find the inspiration to aspire to reach your own goals, however unattainable you may perceive them to be. You were made for so much more, and as my late husband used to say, "Life doesn't give you do-overs." So if you are reading this book and you are in the midst of a life storm, keep pushing forward. Choose to bounce and not break. Never worry or go it alone. Reach out to others, even if you reach out to a stranger on the other side of a phone help line. Chances are by letting others help, you are helping them as well.

This book is for those who persevere despite the setbacks life brings. We find what we are really made of and discover our greatest strengths when the hits just keep coming to knock us down but fail to keep us down. Always imagine yourself falling forward. And with the exception of looking back to recall wisdom from the difficult lessons learned, try not to dwell too much on the past. After all, your past is not where you are going. Unless looking back can help you share with others the lessons you've learned, be selective of where you choose to "cast your pearls." Some people may not be ready to accept your advice, and you need to accept that and move on. Try not to hold grudges. It only drains you of the energy you need to get through the next storm.

They say, "Everything has a season." Well, imagine this season to be your season of growth. After all, even a seedling cannot sprout with growth without being able to first bear the weight of the ground placed on it. Once you adjust your thoughts, your mind and body follow. This is your season, and I am honored that you picked up my book in the midst of it. I will share with you how my God blessed me with the most painful loss, but one I would not trade for anything because it brought me the greatest privilege to serve alongside my hero, my best friend, my husband, a modern-day warrior, a civil servant, a friend to many, a brother to more, and a defender of our freedom.

I've heard said that a hero cannot be made while he is living. Maybe that is because we as humans sometimes fail in openly accepting the greatness of others because of our own insecurities, doubt, envy, or unbelief. Perhaps we do so to project our own weaknesses or our nature to compete rather than collaborate. Or perhaps we sometimes let our pride get in the way.

Just as seasons come and go, the same is said of people. They come in our lives for a season to help us along with the challenge during that period. If they are no longer around—though their absence may take us by surprise—and if we can trust in the maker of the universe, in the end we will come forth from the trial stronger, wiser, and better equipped for the subsequent challenge ahead. Troubles never last, or so they say. I for one sure wish they would, but I guess it's the experience of forging through so many trials that gets us accustomed to continue fighting. Still, the human part of us does have a 100 percent chance of ultimately coming to an end. It is what we choose to do with the time in between that makes us each so unique.

Some theorize that our DNA is created with a preset clock that determines how long we will experience our existence in the physical realm. Last I heard, the leading theory was that a human has the innate capacity to live 110 years. I'm not sure if that still holds, but I do know that ten months before my husband's death, I had a dream that I was climbing a steep mountain. I was wearing the same uniform my husband had on. He was already at the top of the steep cliff. There were about thirty feet between us. I saw him take the last step to reach the top before someone pushed him from the back when he was not looking. My husband fell to his death. The same person who pushed him off was the one who gave me the hand to catch my balance as I reached the same spot. I asked the man in the same uniform why he did it. In my dream I was hoping it was an accident. But the man's face became that of a demon. I woke up in a cold sweat. I still do not know the meaning of the dream or if it was just a sign that I ate too much for dinner the night before.

My husband was a good man. He always impressed his higher ranking officers and employers because he had such a knack for integrating and getting along with people from all walks of life. In a way we were a lot alike but worlds apart. I never really got to know him completely. He used to joke around and tell his friends that he was my "case study." As I write this book, 763 days after Gregory's death by suicide, I am still determined to find the beauty God said He would give me for the ashes. I do not know how much time is on my preset clock; however, I want to leave this world a better place, and I do not want my Gregory's death to be in vain.

In this book you will read my truth as I perceive it. Some names and identifiers have been changed to preserve privacy, dignity, integrity, and honor—the human rights we all are born with. I can only speak for myself, and now that my husband is not around to defend his side, I am committed to speak the truth, however painful it may seem. If something in my account strikes a chord and you disagree, I apologize in advance for my humanness. My intention is not to offend anyone. My mission is noble, and my heart is pure. I do understand that despite the pain of major life trials, we ultimately have the choice to choose our reaction. We can settle into anger or despair for an infinite time with unattainable limits of sorrow that can further drain our body's immune system and the environment we create for those trying to love us. Or we can release the pain and let it go, knowing that if God holds our future and nothing takes Him by surprise, then we can overcome any challenge life brings. I want to use this platform as an opportunity to shed light on the truth. I do not know how many who are reading this book have actual connections to people who chose to take their own lives, but pain is pain. Regardless of the cause, the manifestation of pain is individually experienced, and in the end, we have to endure it so that we can move forward in life. I know sometimes the truth hurts and is better left unsaid until we're in a more appropriate time or place, but I guess that is why a book can be so powerful. Reading a book comes with the added luxury of tossing it, not reading it, or using it for target practice if the information in it is of no use. Writing the book comes with the opportunity to bring voice to the thoughts from deep within without interruption. In this book I will speak my truth, and you can exercise your freedom to agree or disagree.

The absence of my husband left me questioning my purpose. I went from the wife of a hero to a widow that society was not ready to embrace. Many have their opinions of suicide as "a coward's way out." I for one could never do what my Gregory did. Of course, you probably do not know all that I know, and even if you did, it still cannot fully rationalize or justify the taking of an innocent life. Indeed, if you were one of his coworkers from that night and/or one his comrades, you probably know more. Having worked some time in a correctional facility, I had grown accustomed to being on a "need to know" basis. So after Gregory's suicide, I tempered my initial discontent with the chain of command in control and hoped justice would eventually be served and that I would be briefed on the events that had occurred on that dreaded day when my husband was confronted with the news that would tear his world and soul apart.

I have replayed the memory of my last embrace. And instead of going around the same mountain of self-blame, doubt, pity, uncertainty, sorrow, and loss, I have chosen to take a different turn and sing a different tune. I now realize that I am not the only one who has suffered and had to endure unforeseen tragedies. The option to make a choice other than self-loathing is available for you as well. The bumps and potholes, though present and uncomfortable, can at least give us a chance to reach a different perspective. When Gregory was around and I had difficult times in deciding what step to take, he would answer my what-if skepticism with something like, "Sweetie, what if caterpillars had machine guns? The birds wouldn't mess with them." We are all capable of our own responses to life's unpredictable challenges. We can see the glass half full or half empty, or we can just appreciate that we have a glass.

It is surreal how even in his absence I still have his words of wisdom, courage, integrity, and honor to keep me going. During his deployments or trainings away from home, if I was going through a trial at work or in my studies, he would say, "Sweetie, if it were easy, everyone would be a doctor." One of his favorite sayings to inspire me when life was not going well was "Embrace the suck" or "Lean into it." He was right about a lot of things. I did not like the way he undermined himself for not pursuing a higher education. He joked with me and said stuff like, "You have enough degrees for both of us. More degrees than a thermometer." When he said things like that, I always used to tell him that he had learned in life what most never do despite their degrees.

He used to tell me that he was probably never going to make it to heaven because of the "war and what I've done." I used to tell him that he was trained to defend his country from the evil. But even then my late husband had significant difficulty processing and rationalizing whatever tragic memories he had to deal with. He never offered to speak about them, and I never pried. He made the load he carried look easy. Some people are not as talkative, and with him, I am not sure if it would have made a difference. His silence spoke volumes. He had my utmost trust and was worthy of it. Indeed, to his last day, he never gave me reason to doubt his fidelity. After all, he was a proud marine. *Semper fi.*

Seasons of drought and discomfort do not last forever, and that is why I decided to write this book amidst my storm. My hope is that while coming through mine, I can offer some words of encouragement to help you through yours. Perhaps even help you avoid the pitfalls I took so you can at least brace for the blow or steer clear of succumbing to the same mistakes. I guess if we take the lessons learned from our errors, then that, too, in itself can help us as a society to move forward. For example, I never knew that the rate of suicide among soldiers and police officers was so high. I was married to a man whose identity was enmeshed with both. I took it for granted and assumed that because he was part of two large organizations—the military and law enforcement—he was being cared for. He trained me to accept that my physical safety was my responsibility. But I did not know that I needed to share with him that his mental health was his responsibility. My training taught me how to set limits and boundaries with demands from employers, patients, their families, and third-party payers. I was secure in my ignorance that my husband was being taken care of, and I further rationalized any close involvement with his *feelings* because of my own medical training. As a physician, it is not recommended to treat members of your own family. Not only do we medical doctors make awful patients, but at times we cannot make clear judgements when it comes to treating our own family members either. I would like to look back and say that despite the latter, I missed the signs. But in retrospect, there were none. Gregory's suicide took a lot of people by surprise, especially those of us closer to him. He loved his life and his job to protect and serve.

They say there are two kinds of suicides—those with signs and those without. Well, Gregory was at the top of his game and gave no indication of being suicidal. We did not have financial problems. We had the usual debt like the home mortgage, vehicle payments, and my medical and undergraduate school loans. He would describe the latter by saying, "Sweetie, they are *our* loans." We lived within our means. We only went out to dinner once a month. We did our own yard work and cleaning and kept our cost of living down. I was an avid coupon collector and knew how to show up at the grocery stores on the days that had extra deals. We had our occasional slips in spending like when I just had to have the pair of dress shoes I never even got to wear. And there was one major discovery I made with Gregory and his yearly birthday gift to me.

Our birthdays fell within one week of each other. He knew I loved a clean vehicle. So for my birthday, he would personally detail my vehicle from the inside out. It was awesome. I used to look forward to my birthday just so I could have a clean, shiny vehicle outside and inside. He used to be all sweaty when I got home from work, and he would have eaten my box of chocolate. (Well, half eaten. Let me clarify. Most of the pieces were bitten in half because he loved tasting every single one. It was actually a blessing because I did not have to guess what the filling would be inside, and I never minded sharing calories because I wanted to stay fit for him.) He would always have a birthday card for me. Then he would say something like, "Okay, sweetie, I cleaned all three vehicles." (We each had a truck, and he got to bring his police cruiser home, so it really looked like a lot of work for someone to do on a day off.) He would happily add, "You can pick wherever you want to go for dinner, but I'm thinking *blank* or *blank*." Of course, I knew to select one of his preferences because I just so loved to be with him that it really did not matter where we ate. One day I found the vehicle's detailing bill in the glove compartment of my truck and handed it to him. He just smiled and said, "Sweetie, you didn't think I did all that work by myself, did you?" We loved to laugh but never at the expense of each other. We lived within our economic earnings. I saw how difficult it was for him to work those long hours on his details that I made it my priority not to go over our budget.

Gregory was so unique and special to me. He was my prince, my modern-day knight. Though he often joked about himself as being my "special case study," I used to tell him that I was special too. When I did something really dumb like back into something (like the garage), he would say, "Yes, you are special, sweetie, the kind that rides in the special yellow bus." He was able to defuse my biggest worries. "It's just a truck, sweetie. We can get it fixed. No worries." We were compatible— not perfect but just perfectly right for each other. He hated tomatoes, but he loved ketchup. I loved tomatoes and always gave him my extra ketchup. Gregory used to put ketchup on just about everything, even his eggs. But on one particular outing, I was frustrated by something. (I do not even remember what it was.) He was trying to make me smile, so he put a fry on each side of his mouth. He pointed them up, pretended to be a boar, and then ate them. Then he put two more fries facing down and pretended to be a walrus. I did not laugh, not until a couple carrying a baby walked by our table. The baby laughed out loud with such joy at Gregory's performance.

After his funeral one of Gregory's firefighter friends told me how Greg often dropped by just to socialize. On one occasion, he stopped by the firehouse with a gift for his marine friend who had just passed all his requirements and finally made it in as the new firehouse resident. It was a poster that read, "Police officers, God's gift to firefighters so they, too, can have heroes."

Gregory's suicide took many by surprise. We never saw it coming. He loved his job and the soldiers he mentored, led, and cared for. Outside of episodic, intermittent bouts of chewing tobacco, he did not have addiction problems. He loved his country and always said he would have preferred to have "a warrior's death." About three weeks before his death, we drove past our town's police department. They had a police cruiser with a black canvas covering its front windshield. It was done in honor of the police officer who had died. I recall the moment as if it were yesterday. Stopped at the red light in front of the police station, my husband turned to me and broke the silence by saying in a sincere tone, "Sweetie, you never, ever, ever, ever have to worry about me doing that to you. I will never do that to you." Indeed, the police officer's widow contacted me after my husband's funeral and said my husband had paid her a visit to offer her his help. That was my Gregory. He had survived multiple close calls during our times together, and I am sure he survived many others before we ever met.

During his US Marine Corps service while he was stationed in Washington, DC, he volunteered with the Prince County Fire Department. When I met him, he still had the Tasmanian devil that he had worn on his helmet during a rough fire. The latter earned him the rights to ride with his firefighter men. Gregory did not give me the details about the actual heroism in the blaze but did share how his African-American brothers finally accepted him after that call.

I remember two weeks before the suicide, Gregory had just had his cruiser returned from a close call with a drunk driver that sideswiped him and fled the scene. The crash came right after he had an even closer call with an armed man who was fleeing a domestic incident. From what I heard on the news (which I now know is not always reliable), the driver, a former police officer himself, was armed and trying to leave the parking lot. Gregory had to fire some rounds from his shotgun to disable the vehicle. The man almost ran him over. Gregory was a marksman, and he was skilled in firearms. I still believe he could have gotten a clean hit if he had really wanted. He was relieved the vehicle was disabled and the man unharmed.

Gregory was not one to discuss work-related events at home with me. I am pretty sure it was because he did not want me to worry. I guess even though I tried not to show that side of myself, perhaps I failed. I know I prayed for him through multiple tours of duty, details, and deployments, and it shredded me inside when I received the news that he had taken his own life. I still do not understand why suicide elicits so much anger in others. I know a lot of people were and still are quite angry at him. I could not be. I could not because I knew how much he loved his life, his job, and his role as a protector of the innocent. He was a marksman, a trained warrior skillful in defending those of us who run from terror or threats. After his suicide I found I was disappointed with everyone, myself included. I felt he was betrayed. Then I realized that was unproductive. Maybe people were angry because that was the only way they could process the unexpected loss they had no control or power to undue.

As I write this book, I am not pointing the finger. I think that for me, my husband's suicide has been the most difficult challenge I have ever had or ever want to face. I do not wish this on anyone. I so often replay that final day and have to catch myself and reprogram my thoughts to avoid the "I should haves." *I should have done this. I should have done that.* I am not judging anyone. If anything, I have had to forgive everyone, including myself. This book is not about the blame game. I rest in the solace of knowing that my husband survived deployments to war zones and numerous tours of duty as a law enforcement official ultimately succumbing to his own choice. I am a bit scattered in attempting to write because of the charged emotion still within me. Therefore, I forewarn you, the reader, as I leave one topic for another so that I can defuse myself and eventually continue.

You see, I loved my husband and took a vow in front of my God to honor and cherish him until death. Yet even after his death I am now left confused about that love that still continues. I loved him to a point I didn't know I was capable of. It was almost like I knew all along that someday he would not be here. So I would not want one day to go by without him knowing that I loved him. And he at times would acknowledge me and notice my love for him. That would always make me feel so good. He would say something like, "Sweetie, you love me so much. Why?" Because of the inherent danger of his line of work, we both knew every day he came home safe "with the same number of holes and no extra ones," it was a blessing. I would help him in every way I could. I used to love helping him shine his work boots. We always knew when he'd be getting in a foot chase. Curiously, it usually followed the times we shined the boots perfectly. When I saw him put in an extra plate in his bulletproof vest, I used to ask him what-if scenarios. He told me, "It's all in your mind. You program yourself to fight to come home, no matter what." He taught me to program myself if ever I was in a life or death situation to "just tell yourself you are coming home." He always had entertained my what-if scenarios. And, when he did not know the answer, he would admit to it. "I'm not sure. Let's Google it."

Gregory was a simple yet complex man. He loved animals, especially his special rescue dogs and cats. I remember once I told him about the walk the dog and I took in a wooded area. The sun had set earlier than usual, and our dog, a long-haired German shepherd, and I were caught in the dark. I heard leaves rustling and noticed the hair on the back of Beckett's neck and shoulder blades sticking up. I focused on the place where he was sniffing and saw four sets of yellow eyes in the woods. They stood about knee high from where we were standing. As we approached, the dog started a growl I had never heard. The eyes in the brush appeared to move in a synchronous semicircle. *Hmmm*, I thought like the warrior princess my husband had trained me to be. *Retreat.* Sometimes backing up and taking a different turn is not as bad as some make it sound. In our defense, we never actually turned around. We just walked backward. When I got home and asked him about the scenario, he said, "Sweetie, if a wild, rabid coyote is going to attack you, give him your left forearm, and when he bites you, shoot him in the throat with your right hand." I thought he was serious. I am glad to admit I still have not gotten the opportunity to test out his theory.

The stories I shared with him never came close to the ones I read about in the police newsletter about my chivalrous husband. I still have a scrap book full of them. His grandparents and aunt helped me collect them. I never felt the need to compete with him for anything. I loved being in the sidelines. I was his biggest fan. When he deployed, I was honored to "hold the fort" until his return. The postal workers knew me by first name because I mailed my husband a care package every week. I loved loving him. He was my pride. He gave meaning, purpose, security, and value to my life. We used to joke about the pay difference of our jobs. He had to work three to four hours to make what I did in one. Because we did not have children, I used to support his decision to take the holiday shifts so that his comrades could have time with theirs. It was okay because we spent good quality time together and avoided the holiday crowds, and we could celebrate the holidays as his schedule permitted. My life revolved around him, and I am so guilty of being okay with it. I was proud to be his wife and did not mind waiting for him to return home whether he was in the States or abroad. Perhaps that is why it was especially challenging to regain my footing after his death.

Part of the reason I needed to write this book was to give hope. I lost my identity when I lost him. I never knew so much love and so much pain. It literally left me almost lifeless. The days and months that followed were a blur. I journaled, and I began running on a treadmill. I started with an almost twenty-minute mile. I figured from my education that Gregory's death would surely deprive me of the serotonin and other naturally made brain chemicals. So God gave me the grace to test my own theory of restoring them in a socially acceptable manner. I knew about the runners' high. So the day after his passing, I took to the treadmill. I remember having to hold the rails as I jogged to keep from falling because I sobbed as I ran. I now run four miles in less than thirty minutes (but I still hold on to the rails). I am not bragging, or maybe I am. I still cannot fully appreciate the benefit from the accomplishment, but I am still trying. I think he would be proud if he saw how I kept moving forward, even if it is one small step at a time.

As I write, the statistics keep growing. Being a law enforcement officer carries three times the risk of suicide, and being in the military, I am sure, does not make that any easier. Still, while he was in my life, I was able to appreciate all the times he came home. We grew able to not take each other for granted. He gave me a kiss on the forehead every time he left home and a kiss on the lips every time he returned. I so miss him, but now God has graced me with the ability to appreciate the memory of a rare privilege.

My identity was bound up as his wife. And when he was gone, it was like life just took the wind out of me. I lost my core. I felt I had failed him because I had not been enough to hold him safe from the world's tempestuous storms. With his death, my purpose in life was gone. The weeks that followed were awful. It was like rehabilitation and learning to live again. The simple things—grocery shopping (for one), laundry, cooking, cleaning, even the toothbrush (just one)—were such challenges. I hated to hear, "Oh, you'll be fine. Just help someone else. It'll just take some time." Well, about that. I'm still waiting and trying to learn how to help someone else, and I'm even learning how to adjust the way I pray.

Most of my prayers were for him and those he worked with and protected. And if you are reading this book and someone has told you, "You'll be fine. The pain will go away," do not fret if you continue to feel the sting. I know I still do feel the pain. For me it has not gone away. Indeed, my experience has been quite different. I still have not been able to reach my new baseline. I will admit that may have something to do with my own choices and my refusal to let go of it. I still choose to have the pain. It is almost as if I need to carry it for a little while longer until I can use it to fuel my campaign of exonerating him and all those like him. Their blood cries from the earth to warn us that as a society we need to do more to protect those who put their lives on the line for our freedom. "Freedom is not free, sweetie." That's what he used to tell me.

I would pray for him and his comrades and coworkers every morning and every night. In retrospect, I now realize my prayers were kind of dumb. (I was praying for what had already been granted in Psalm 91, which I committed to memory). My prayers often included requests that God would send His angels to keep them safe from the evil. Gregory had a separate body armor plate that he would place in front of his heart under the expired bulletproof vest his job issued him. When my husband's preset clock stopped, it left me so confused. In the end, no one captured or tortured him. No evil cowardly terrorist took him hostage. No drunk driver ran him over or rear-ended him, and no runaway convict shot him from behind or took him by surprise. Despite my faith in God, my husband's harm was always my biggest fear. I am not sure if how he died made accepting of his death any easier. And though I know I risk being judged for what I am about to disclose as my truth, the fact is that my husband made a decision. No one took his life, but he gave it.

He laid down his life to avoid the perception of tarnishing the reputation of the brethren who wore the same uniform with similar badges. In an effort to quiet the scandalous rumors that were sure to follow, he chose to solve the problem his own way. I guess given the options, he made a choice based on his risk-and-benefit assessment. Unlike the suicide bombers or jihadists who callously and cowardly take their lives with reckless disregard for innocent parties and the collateral damage, at least my husband's suicide resulted in the physical taking of only his.

He purchased a firearm specifically for the purpose of taking his own life. I suppose he chose the bullet, and from the letter he wrote me, he was fully aware that his decision would impact those who at one point truly loved respected and admired him. He apologized for "taking the coward's way out." Yes, I do question whether he would have made a different choice had he been given alternatives. But in the end, I know there is nothing I can do, say, or think to bring him back. I cannot change or undo his decision. And as recommended in Romans 14, I dare not judge. My hope is that in my transparence I can offer some sort of alternative to anyone who may be contemplating the same destination. There is hope. There's always hope. There are unfortunate circumstances that happen to all of us regardless of our accomplishments and achievements. There will always be a risk in taking chances for the advancement of careers. My husband used to reassure me with his usual statement, "Sweetie, everything I do, I do because I love you." I know he was innocent at the time of his death. It does not matter how others see him. To me, he will always be my hero. It pains me greatly to know that society saw him as a hero one day and a nobody the next.

My husband was a war-decorated veteran. If you go online and look up Sergeant Gregory Jasinskas, you will have the option to go to a site called Together We Served. There are more medals listed on the site, and I know he would never brag about himself; however I will now take the opportunity to list a few of his awards before his last deployment.

- Bronze Star Medal
- Army Commendation Medal
- Army Achievement Medal
- Navy/Marine Corps Achievement Medal
- Navy/Marine Corps Meritorious Unit Commendation (third)
- Army Good Conduct Medal
- Marine Corps Good Conduct Medal (second)
- Army Reserve Components Achievement Medal
- National Defense Service Medal (second)
- Korean Defense Service Medal
- Army Overseas Service Ribbon
- Navy/Marine Corps Sea Service Deployment Ribbon
- Navy/Marine Corps Overseas Service Ribbon (second)
- Armed Forces Reserve Medal (second)
- Global War on Terrorism Service Medal
- Iraq Campaign Medal
- Army Service Ribbon

Ironically, his favorite and most cherished award did not come from our country's military. It was a hand-etched plaque from the newly formed police command he helped organize. He was awarded the honor by the newly elected police chief himself. Therefore, did come to me as a surprise when I met with my husband's boss (from his civilian law enforcement job here in the United States). The boss had personally come to my house to extend his apologies for the inability of his officers to "show presence at the funeral." I had God on my side and knew the messenger sent to deliver the unfortunate message was just that, a messenger. I thanked him for the visit and went downstairs. I put my boxing gloves on, the ones Gregory had gotten me for my birthday, and I just punched the punching bag until I was too exhausted to think. The following day, I found a notebook from one of Gregory's deployments where he listed "four types of threats." They were written in his handwriting, suggesting that he was either in a lecture or taking notes for a mission. But the heading followed the caption "Biggest Enemy: Time and Place Predictability." The threats were listed as *assassination*, *kidnapping*, *injury*, and the final one, *embarrassment*. Many of his mission briefs referred to the person or object to be protected as the *principle*. Well, in my opinion, his department took the word of an unreliable source over the exemplary track record of a dedicated, war-decorated, reputable employee, and the results left my husband alone to face the embarrassment that would surely follow. I think Gregory chose to "fall on his sword" instead of facing the horrific shameful scene that would undoubtedly follow. I am in no way saying that suicide is the way to go. I will not judge him, especially given the fact that I did not have to walk in his shoes and did not know what load he had been carrying from everything he had experienced as early as seventeen years old. I wish I had the answers to why people, soldiers, and law enforcement officials decide to take their own lives. But I do not. I know suicide in general is a topic that is no respecter of persons and has been the unfortunate destination for many regardless of race, ethnicity, profession, education level, socioeconomic status, and age.

Gregory was raised a particular religion, and I had a friend from that religion tell me that some believe that God gives humans a choice. The source said that perhaps Gregory made his. It is interesting. In my read of Deuteronomy 30:19, I believe the passage says to "choose life." Regardless, of what we individually choose to focus on, the choice is made on an individual basis in the end. My hope through this book is that despite honoring my husband for his many acts of courage and valor, suicide will not be an option for you. Yes, I survived his loss, but my husband chose a permanent solution for a temporary problem. And I do not cast judgement on his final choice. I still love and miss him dearly. And I wish to God he would not have made the decision. Neither he nor my God consulted me in what was to unfold. And just as his family and friends, I was left with an emotional scar and a lot of questions that are still unanswered. My hope is that anyone struggling with a seemingly irreversible challenge will choose to live.

My husband used to end his e-mails an Edmund Burke quote that says, "The only thing necessary for the triumph of evil is for good men to do nothing." This book is for the good in all of us. It is for the comeback kid in all of us, the one who can't be kept down. The good thing about falling so often is that bouncing back up eventually becomes a reflex. We have learned that life's setbacks are really setups for propelling us forward to new seasons with higher levels of strength, courage, and expectation. This book is dedicated to all who have had to deal with the unfortunate collateral damage that follows suicide. It is especially written for the families of the men and women in law enforcement, the military, and fire departments. This book is for those who continue to sacrifice their time, relationships, and energies so that others can have freedom. It is for those who truly understand that freedom is everything but free.

9/11

"Funny story" is how he would start his recollections of mishaps, miracles, and tales of unbelievable situations only he and his wild angels could find themselves in. For example, there's the story of how he learned to speak his Spanish. He says he was guarding a US embassy in Liberia. The natives there thought it was a good idea on that one hot day to charge the embassy "for no real reason." My husband, then a young US Marine sergeant, gave the verbal warning and followed his orders by the book. But the natives kept charging. Well, my husband was a man of few words. He proudly told me the words he was taught that day by his fellow marines. Among the marines with him on that tour, there were a few who had originally been born and raised in Southern California. They took pride in their Mexican-American heritage, and Gregory told me they showed great courage in battle. The words they taught him, however, were not ones you could repeat in front of your grandmother or mine. I did not have the heart to tell my husband the truth about the translation. I just politely asked him to please not repeat it in front of my family.

The embassy was protected that day, and all was well on the US territory and with its inhabitants. It was stories like that, ones with no real specifics of the collateral damage or toll that marked the bulk of my life as the wife of a modern-day warrior and hero. I had a lot of questions that I was unable to ask out of respect for his privacy and his need to remain in control of the situation and what he chose to disclose.

I respected him for what he had seen, experienced, and endured during his many tours as a marine, a military police officer, a federal police officer, and as a state trooper. We had come from totally different worlds. Yet as my husband would say, "We all bleed red." There was a particular account that I never got the chance to ask him about. It happened in the early 90s and involved two helicopters carrying US Marines off the coast of Hawaii. There had been a reported accident where eleven US Marines were killed instantly because of faulty equipment. Rumor had it that it was Gregory's men. He had stayed behind to help the slower marine. Within minutes, both choppers went down. I imagine Gregory carried a lot of those untold stories in his memory. He chose not to share them with me because of reasons only he knew. He may have blamed himself or carried survivor's guilt, but he never disclosed that to me either. What I do know is that after 9/11, he did not think twice before reenlisting. Despite our differences, Gregory and I had a lot in common. I, too, wanted to volunteer after 9/11. He used to tell me, "Sweetie, one uniform is enough in the family." We were from different worlds, but we shared that commitment to our homeland.

Gregory had been raised in an upper-middle-class family. His father had been an affluent engineer with expertise in aviation. (I think that, too, was always a mystery neither he nor his family chose to discuss). His father's career led him to exotic places yet required major sacrifices, so he was absence from the family for lengthy periods. I suppose that is how Gregory's mother refined her strength, raising Gregory and his younger sister during all those times Gregory's father was called away for his work. They wanted Gregory to avoid a military career despite the fact that he was a third-generation servant of Uncle Sam. At seventeen years of age, Gregory stood his ground by telling his parents that he would not be traveling to Asia with the new assignment his father had earned as a promotion. My husband announced to his parents he was staying in the United States, living with his grandparents, and looking into becoming one of those few good men the US Marine Corps were recruiting.

My upbringing was the total opposite. While Gregory spent his childhood as a Boy Scout, I spent mine as a migrant farmworker. However, as one of the youngest members in a family of eight, there were certain cultural expectations that my parents and I also came to prioritize differently. My parents emigrated from Mexico during their early childhood years. While they adopted the conservative socialization of their native land and culture, I strived as a youth toward one of my own. They had big expectations for me to earn an honorable life via manual labor. This would exclude the pursuit of a higher education and include an arranged marriage at an early age, and I would raise at least five children of my own. It was the rebel in me that was attracted to the disciplined warrior in Gregory. While my parents adopted the tradition of legal marriage following a fully chaperoned courtship as required by *mis abuelos*, I chose to stay in school and graduate. It took great mental courage to break that tradition.

My grandparents joined in the journey of relocating *la familia* to the United States when my parents were in their early childhood years. Legend has it that my father's dad was a horse rancher. He supplied horses for the Mexican Federales. One day a high-appointed official from the Mexican Army came to Grandpa's horse ranch and demanded the sale of my granddaddy's favorite white horse. "That one is not for sale," said *abuelito* humbly. But the official was not taking no for an answer. He instead threatened to take the white palomino for pay or leave him dead. He gave my grandfather the choice. My grandfather was said to be a noble man of great strength and courage, one who was quick to draw. The latter resulted in the death of the Mexican authority figure. It was clear before sundown on that day that evil would prevail. In one second the lives of many were changed. One second is all it took, and another widow was made. My grandfather reflexively drew his weapon, killing the Mexican official, and thereby, he ended both lifelong careers. My grandfather had to seek life on the run in northern Mexico. He lived as an outcast for two years in the forest and was said to have been on the run until a distant cousin of his was elected president, granting my grandfather asylum and permission to return to reclaim his property and business. It was then that my grandfather decided to relocate to the United States. His first wife had died during the birth of his youngest son. As is tradition, for the year my grandfather mourned the death of his first wife, wearing the black armband. The irony is that during the burial of my husband, the agency did not permit my husband's brothers-in-arms to wear the black band around their badges or even to attend in uniform. But I digress. My grandfather remarried, and my father was second to the youngest from that second marriage.

My father arrived in the United States at five years old. Unlike Gregory's father, my dad was not an engineer. My father was illiterate. He never completed grade school. Neither of my parents did. I was raised being told that my destiny was to live the life of poverty like Jesus did. I never really understood or accepted that and instead chose to believe John 10:10, which reads, "I have come that they have life and have it more abundantly."

Despite our differences today, even though both sets of grandparents are no longer physically present, their presence continues to be a part of my life through their traditions. Gregory's grandfather died during one of his last tours. It was sad to see Gregory arrive midway into his deployment. He was one to defer those midtour visits home because to him it was more of a stressor leaving his younger comrades in the line of fire. Gregory's grandfather was such an awesome person. He and Grandma had been married for a long time—more than sixty years. Gregory loved his grandfather dearly. He had returned from a prior deployment and had to see his father lose his battle to cancer. I remember the solemn quietness during the funeral we attended together for his father. It is surreal to think about how many funerals and wakes I attended with Gregory. Being the wife of a military serviceman who just so happens to also be in law enforcement brings with it that added risk. Gregory had numerous friends who were also firefighters, and Gregory always volunteered to escort the funeral procession. Most of the times, police escorts attend. This is done on a voluntary basis and only after they secure approval from their departments. Gregory had to go through the death of his father, and I am sure that was no easy task, especially for his mother. After all, they had been married for forty years. From watching Gregory's mother deal with the loss, I learned how to show strength despite inner pain.

Gregory displayed much of the same inner strength upon his arrival home for Papa's funeral. The Red Cross notified him of his grandfather's death. Gregory's preference had been to opt out of returning home for the funeral. Yet his upper chain of command granted him the leave. It was quite a trial to endure. Though I was reassured by seeing him physically present for the brief visit, we in no way could express any kind of joy or celebration for his return. Gregory always held his soldiers and their safety as a paramount priority. He had left them behind in a war zone to bid farewell to his deceased grandfather. Gregory was thankful to show support to his widowed grandmother, who was into her early years of dementia. Grandma still gave strong *rompe huesos abrazos* (hugs so strong they could break bones). But she sent him back to war with that blank stare she developed as the dementia progressed. That also must have been difficult for him to endure. I remember the frequent visits over to Grandma's house. She would cut out job advertisements and would have them lined up on her kitchen table to review with Gregory during our visits. Watching would always give me a sorrowful feeling. Gregory would take the cutouts and the coupons for cat litter she had also gathered for him. When Papa was living, he would clip out the numerous newspaper articles about his grandson. I actually started a scrapbook that I still have today. He called it part of his "I love me" collection.

During one of Gregory's deployment, I was at my residency program in the emergency room and saw a copy of the *Herald*. It had a picture of Gregory in Baghdad, and it was snowing! That was funny to me because in an effort to stay focused on the home front while he went off for his deployments, I had to avoid watching the news. And yet on this day when I particularly missed him and prayed God to send me a sign that he was well, I was blessed by seeing his face on the front page of the paper.

I had met my husband when I was an intern. As a first-generation Mexican-American, negotiating a higher education was no easy feat. I finally made it through medical school and into my first-choice residency training program. Actually, it was the only choice I listed. And to this day, I cannot really understand that choice. I figured at that time that I had become familiar with the local teaching systems and wanted to leave unnecessary unknowns out of the learning equation. Being a single female in a large city had its own challenges. Besides, as a migrant farm worker, I had done my share of traveling down the East Coast, following the tomato crops. We had to travel to five different states during the academic year. It became quite an educational disruption but a blessing at the same time. Yet the other deciding factor in my choice for residency training was money. As an entering intern, I had scarce funds. So I had to rely on public transportation. I had the unfortunate experience on one crowded subway trip of being groped, and when I went to report the incident, I guess the offender was well known to the transit police. Regardless, I chose to walk when I could. It was during one of those walks that my eyes first caught glimpse of my sweetie.

He was transitioning out of the US Marines, serving in the US Marine Corps inactive ready reserves and working as a police officer with US Veterans Affairs. I found out that the latter was not the same as *security officer*, even though the doorway to his office clearly stated, "Security." Gregory clarified that he was a federal police officer, and as such, he was licensed to carry in every state. Nice. I did not really appreciate that distinction. To me, a person in a uniform that had some sort of badge or official patch was symbolic of authority and respect. I would see my *flaco huero* (skinny, light-skinned friend) during my walks to the VA. I would often see him writing bright orange sticker tickets and gluing them on the dashboards of the illegally parked vehicles. The shiny polished Mercedes, Audis, Jaguars, and BMWs in the handicapped spaces were no match for the federal police officer who swiftly tagged five in a row. It was awesome! I would go for my shift in the emergency room and hear all the nurses and doctors complain about the tickets they found on their windshields. Now, that to me was hilarious. I thought, *Why do they choose to park in a handicapped space when there is a garage twenty feet away?* I think I fell in love that first day, but of course, I did not disclose it. Midway into my internship, I had made it on a locked inpatient psychiatric ward. There was an unfortunate occurrence on my first day. One of the patients had a flashback of Vietnam. He mistook the nurse for the enemy. I was standing in the nurse's station, and the patient pushed me and shouted, "It's the enemy. *It's the enemy!*" The Vietnam veteran pulled out his intravenous line, and as my back hit the wall and set off the emergency alarm, I watched him wrap the IV line around the nurse's neck. As blood poured out and I fell to the ground, the corner of my eye caught the federal police officer move swiftly through three locked doors. In one fell swoop, he swiftly grabbed the vet's hand and loosened the hold on the nurse's neck. "It's okay, buddy. The coast is clear. I got you now. Everything is okay." That's all I heard as he calmly escorted the veteran out of the nurse's station. I was kind of in shock. What raced through my mind was the violence I had seen as a child during those moves into crowded housing. I am not sure how long I was on the floor. I sure was embarrassed. And as I sat there, trying to recuperate and ground myself, I saw a hand. It was his. "You okay, doc?"

Well, months later I saw him in the elevator. I was completing an overnight shift, monitoring eighty patients. He was just starting his ticket-issuing mission. He said good morning as I walked out of the elevator. I had just had a bad night. One of the patients had a drop in his hematocrit, the equivalent of losing three pints of blood. But I said, "No one dies on Maria's shift." That was my motto. In an effort to hold to the commitment I had made with God when I was granted my degree to practice medicine, I never slept during my night float shifts. I would systematically start on one floor at a time, reviewing everyone's labs and doing my rounds on every patient. Well, I came across the patient with the GI bleed because of God's discerning power. I was making my rounds on the last ward and saw a particular elderly male with the international sign of a heart attack. He was pale, and I knew instinctively what was happening. I woke him and told him what the plan was. He responded angrily, "I don't take help from your kind."

"Sir," I answered respectively, "right now I am all you have, and I've written the orders for your immediate transfusion and the medication you need. And you can take up that issue with your attending in the morning." God helped me save that man's life. God used me to keep him alive and prevent another widow's heart break. I was honored to have served in that capacity, and seeing Gregory in the that elevator that morning, his skin color just hurt. It hurt just a little because I didn't know at that point if I would be "his kind." Growing up as a migrant farmworker had exposed me to a lot of racism and poverty and all the unfortunate judgment that went with that lifestyle. We had spent a lot of time homeless, hungry, and without the basic needs of life. Through all the hardships, I never stopped believing God for the better. And now face-to-face with the brave, bald, white man in the elevator, I was armed to meet the challenge. Before I could finish my thought, however, he asked me for my phone number.

Yes, that is exactly how I recall it. I saw the badge on his uniform and wrote the wrong number on the piece of paper I handed him. It was intentional. I did not want to risk rejection. Well, three months later I saw him, and after a lot of praying and fasting about the matter, I walked up to him and gave him a previously written note with the correct phone number and handed it to him. I said, "Here is the real number. I intentionally gave you the wrong number before." (It turns out as he later confessed that he never even dialed it. He had left it in his uniform and washed it.) "What did you think, doc? I just wanted lunch? Did you think I was trying to go out and fall in love and—" We laughed as we somehow managed to complete the sentence together, "Get married and buy a house with a white picket fence and a German shepherd."

"Yes," I continued, still laughing. Three more months went by, and then I finally got the call from him. We had our first date on Valentine's Day. I could not believe my prayers for a knight had finally come to fruition. Of course, I offered to pay for the dinner bill because I did not want to mislead him into thinking I was going to be dessert. We were inseparable in spirit from that day forth. He continued issuing his tickets to the illegally parked patrons of the VA, and I pressed through with my residency training. Then 9/11 happened. He reenlisted and was deployed with the US Marine Corps reserve unit.

After September 11, 2001, it was clear his deployment would eventually arrive. I was somewhat relieved that his unit was not getting deployed. However, he was not. So he transferred to one that eventually did. He had to leave his unit, and he went to the Middle East with the National Guard as part of a military police (MP) company. The MP company was an excellent way for Gregory to shine and use his modern-day warrior skills to train the younger, newly enlisted soldiers who wanted to serve and do their part in the war on terrorism. Gregory would text me when he could. He was not one to hog up the jammed phone or computer lines. He always let his soldiers contact home, especially the ones with the worried moms or kids. I was pretty much okay without verbal contact. I convinced myself that I was going on faith. I had to try to stay positive when days and weeks went by without hearing from him. I knew he would return home safely because that was how I was living my life, expecting and hoping for the best.

I was going to do my part to stand in the gap and support him in the fight for America's freedom. I was determined to be his one-woman cheerleading squad when he did get the chance to call me. I would keep our brief conversations positive, and I would not disclose to him the details about the long, emotionally cold, and lonely days and nights. I avoided letting him in on how awful I felt that we had to be apart. I laughed at all his jokes even when half of them were broken up because of bad connections. I used to hate when that happened because I knew my husband would not take up phone time and would make sure his soldiers got adequate phone time with their loved ones back home. And that was totally fine by me because I knew we were at war and the greater enemy was out there trying to sabotage the freedom and rights of our country and all it stood for. I was fighting in my own way. So even when our short three- to five-minute phone conversations were cut short, I knew I was fighting the good fight by helping keep his morale up. It was not easy. I remember keeping a little notebook where I would prioritize what I needed him to know, and without fail, every time he called, nothing on the notebook made it into the conversation because it really did not matter in the greater scheme. The little things were not worth mentioning when I heard the sound of his voice with the background chanting on the loudspeakers or the bombs and artillery rounds going off.

Redeployment

I am not sure exactly what events during his deployment to the Middle East transpired to result in Gregory's Bronze Star. He was never one to discuss the details of work-related issues. And he surely was one reluctant to brag about the acts of valor displayed in battle. It did not matter to me. I was just so proud and happy that he and his comrades returned home to their families safe and with no extra holes. Gregory was never one to talk about war-related stuff. I did see on one of his notepads that he and his soldiers had successfully completed 121 missions during one deployment and more than two hundred on another. On the day following his suicide, I also received an awe-inspiring phone call from a general expressing his condolences. The brigadier general said, "Mrs. Jasinskas, I had ten thousand troops under my command, but when I needed something done behind the wire, I knew one soldier by name." He said that my husband "would be the one to get it done." The latter was exceptionally therapeutic, especially after the visit from my husband's boss in his civilian job. I am still not blaming the colonel of the law enforcement agency. Even in my darkest hour of despair, God gave me the grace to not point any fingers. It was not how my husband wanted it, and I wanted to honor that special, unique, rare, but valuable trait rarely seen these days. I remember the contrasting colonel's visit to my home after Gregory's suicide. I saw the vehicle in the driveway, and my first thought was of thanksgiving. Perhaps I would be given some answers and told that justice somehow had been served. Instead I was told, "Given the nature of the circumstance, we will not be able to show presence at the funeral." The colonel did not know what I knew, so how could I judge him?

I calmly said, "You were judge, jury, and verdict in one fell swoop. You stripped a war-decorated hero of his honor."

The colonel, who was equally calm, resounded, "I have two thousand troopers under my command. How could I possibly know all of them?"

I do not remember the entire conversation. But I serve under a higher power, and God enabled me to remain calm. I said, "With all due respect, I know your position of power took due diligence, but you took the word of someone who brought the same allegation against an innocent police officer four years earlier. You gave the order to strip my husband of his uniform, his badge, his weapon, and his cruiser. He would have taken a bullet for any one of you. With a slanderous accusation, what did you expect him to do?"

I stopped for sincere concern that something awful could be made worse. I recalled how I had to drive Gregory's tuxedo-black Ford F150 home after his suicide. It was close to the hotel where he stayed the day he shot himself. I imagined but could not fathom the steps my husband had to take to plan and carry out his own death. I remembered the last strong hug he gave me as he drove off the day before. I can still hear his voice, "Sweetie, I'm done. Even though I didn't do what I'm being accused of, even though I'll be found not guilty after the long wait and the trial is over, I will always be 'that guy.' Both of my careers are done. I can't be a criminal investigator if I am being criminally investigated."

The colonel got up from the kitchen chair I had openly offered him. He had nothing to say in response. My husband was dead, and nothing I could say or do at that point could bring him back. Nothing.

As a last-ditch effort of being heard, I said something like, "Something good has to come out of this. Maybe cameras on the dashboards. Maybe a change in protocol." His response was about how it wasn't "cost-efficient." He left my house, and I didn't have answers. I still am. The colonel did not know that my husband had handwritten me a suicide letter that he had dropped in the mailbox hours before he pulled the trigger and took his own life. The colonel did not know that in the letter my husband had specifically requested that I bury him in his civilian uniform—the one he loved so much, the one he would live and die for. Well, the colonel also did not know that my husband was a man of his word. And it did not matter to me what lies the colonel believed. To me, my husband was and is innocent. To this day I do not know what the allegation was.

I will never forget. The colonel got up and walked out. I know he was just doing his job. And my husband would never bad mouth his brethren. As an act of respect, I would not either. But withholding the truth is not in my own personal repertoire. My husband had returned from the Afghanistan deployment a bit disappointed. He was so enthusiastic and satisfied because he and his soldiers had accomplished more than three hundred missions. They had helped establish the police command. Gregory was so proud of the hand-etched plaque given to him by the police department's newly elected chief. Yet there was an awful IED explosion that resulted in the fatal death of the entire unit that had arrived from California. The soldiers and the service animal had been on the bus that was hit by the IED. I remember receiving the phone call. Gregory hardly ever made phone calls home. But he knew the incident would make the five-o'clock news and did not want me to worry. He left the message reassuring me, "Sweetie, I saw some bad stuff happened. I'm okay. We are all okay. We are all alive."

I later received a more detailed e-mail of reassurance. It was not until the end of the deployment that I was able to hear more about what had happened that day. Before knowing what tragedy would later unfold,

Gregory asked for volunteers to accompany him. One soldier accepted his offer. Gregory had taken the young soldier under his wing that day. Of all that occurred, that was his biggest concern, "what he had to see because I brought him with me." Apparently through the conversation I had with my husband, Gregory said the soldier worked hard all day to assist with picking up the remains of the fallen soldiers who had their lives taken so brutally and without even a chance to fight back or defend themselves. The young soldier my husband had taken with him on that day held it together and worked diligently despite the atrocity. In the end, however, his soldier did not receive any formal acknowledgment for his act of valor and courage that day on the battlefield. Instead the medals were awarded to some of the officers who had showed up after the cleanup had been completed. Although my husband would not speak about it, I knew the incident broke my husband's heart.

I had heard much more about the IED explosion on the news. I remember my husband's phone call to reassure me of his safety was brief. However, the detailed account he later shared with me was about the service dog that also lost his life that day. To Americans, our pets are like family. Gregory loved animals. Shortly before his last deployment, I asked if we could start our own family, and rather than give me an answer, he took me on a field trip to the local animal shelter to rescue yet another four-legged friend.

Gregory would have made an awesome father. He told me that he did not want to be absent from the early years of his children's development. So we were planning to start a family after his military obligation was complete. Well, on that dreaded day in October, Gregory said he saw the service dog outside the wire. He always loved to share stories about the service dogs in the military and the stray dogs that befriended the troops. Gregory said earlier that day the unit's service dog, a chocolate Labrador, had somehow gotten away from her handler. "It's like she came to say good-bye." Gregory said he brought the service canine back to its handler about an hour before the scheduled bus ride to the other base.

Gregory told me that while cleaning up the remains from the IED explosion, he was able to hold it together until he saw someone carrying the burned brown fur. He said that was extremely difficult. I suppose he may have felt responsible. Well, it is amazing how powerful of an impact animals can have in our lives. Gregory did not leave me with children to raise. And because he was an only son (born to a father who was also an only son), when my husband died, somehow the pain of knowing that his last name would not be carried over to another generation still struck a deep chord of sorrow within me. It is during those futile moments that I fight mentally to stay positive. Gregory left behind a legacy of love and courage that will live in those he helped, served, mentored, and encouraged.

Family Days

When Gregory would deploy or return home from deployments, he liked to say his good-byes and hellos early, mostly away from the crowds of families that would come to see their loved ones. He told me he did that so I wouldn't have to see so many people crying. Indeed, I would walk away and not look back because I was also eager to begin my "deployment day" countdown. I would journal from deployment day one to deployment day 364. It helped me get through the year(s) we had to be apart. I remember two weeks before his second deployment to the Middle East, he told me, "Sweetie, we have to make this official." We had been engaged for so long, but we never had the time or finances to plan our actual wedding. So he gave me the choice, "You have this weekend or next. Just in case I get taken out, you'll be taken care of." He was referring to the possibility of getting killed in action while he was away. Funny, I never doubted he would return safe because I had enough faith for both of us. But I did not want to miss my chance at officially marrying the man of my dreams. After all, he was my knight in shining armor and my prince. We made the wedding happen with eight hundred dollars on the following weekend.

A couple of my girlfriends pitched in and helped me buy the wedding dress. We spent most of the money on the food for the six couples we invited to the dinner. I still remember the day of our wedding. It was cloudy and rainy, and I remember asking God for sunshine because it was going to be in the backyard of the minister's house. I remember two hours before the rain stopped. It was still cloudy, but I knew by faith that God would provide some sunshine. And sure enough, right before the twenty-minute ceremony, it was like God sneezed to clear the clouds and let the sun shine through. It was awesome. And without knowing, three of the invited women brought their own cameras, and each one gave us a copy of the photos they took in three separate photo albums. I felt so blessed. I still remember how the minister that day held my ring inside Gregory's and said though this did not happened often when the rings fit perfectly inside one another, it had a special meaning reflecting the added strength of the bond of love.

Well, we did not get to go on our honeymoon until Gregory returned from his 365 days away. Although Gregory and his soldiers all returned home safe and in good spirits, I could not help but feel as if I had missed something. Every deployment left me questioning the "in between" time. I had grown to trust my husband. I held his personal time in high reverence, not to mention his work time and the time he needed to spend with his male friends for bonding. Gregory was—and in my mind will always be—a man of honor, integrity, courage, and strength. I never doubted his fidelity. But every time he returned from a deployment, I found myself wanting to smother him. I did everything in my power to avoid acting out those urges. I saw others around him, trying to obtain details from him, and I always tried to make it easier for him so that he didn't have to repeat stories he really did not want to talk about. I would change the subject because I used to love to see him laugh. He made the silliest jokes, and he had such a stern look that whenever funny information came out of his mouth, it just made it even funnier.

One of the family days involved an extremely late return. It was almost midnight when the police-escorted buses drove into the base.

I remember it was late because most of the kids had fallen asleep in the gymnasium. Thankfully, Gregory's friend, the one who had walked me down the aisle to give me away, was kind enough to drive me to the base to meet him. There were no real ceremonies upon our return. It was almost as if unseen tension and unspoken strife dissipated immediately upon reuniting with families. What really was important, what it was all for and what really mattered was present and overpowered any discord that may have formed roots of bitterness. I am sure that while he was away and living in the close proximity to comrades, multiple disagreements and discord resulted. But the air cleared with the love expressed between the returning soldiers and their families.

I remember one of Gregory's returns. Despite the late hour, the company's general came up to me and Gregory with his son. The general sincerely introduced my husband to his son. "Son, this is the man who saved my life." My husband shook the young adolescent's hand, and the general shook mine. My husband never mentioned the actual incident. I still do not know what he was referring to.

I still have a lot of the e-mails he sent me. The following are a few with the dates. Some of the language was modified.

In one of the email dated 3/17/2011, he writes:

> Hey guys, sorry it has taken so long. Been very busy here. We have been in and out of the field. We have done 10 days of mounted gunnery (shooting big guns from trucks) and live fire convoy ops (shooting big guns from moving trucks in groups). Then we came out of the field for a couple of days and went into 4 days of Military Operations on Urban Terrain (MOUT). That is kinda like doing war in the confined spaces of a city. Now we are starting 5 days of IED Defeat. Which is react

to Improvised Explosive Devices. After that we roll into the Command Post Exercise and then Validation. Days are long but the weather has been decent. It is starting to get hot not, 80's but it has been fairly clear. Only rained a couple of times … We are still on target for our ship date. All is well and we are doing pretty good. Just looking to get out of here. I will send an update when we get out of the IED lane. Thanks for all the responses and sorry I haven't been able to get back to you individually as much as I want computer time here is limited. Thanks for all the support!

On an e-mail dated 7/7/2011, he writes,

Hey guys! Been crazy busy here. We had a thing over at headquarters this morning. Got my picture with the General, again! First time was in Baghdad … Things are good. I am out of the wire pretty much every day going here, there, and everywhere. Days are long, but it make the time fly by. Better than sitting around and doing nothing. Getting HOT here. We are usually in the high 90's. Its not bad in the shade, but in the sun it is outta control. So, things are good. I hope everyone is doing well and staying safe. Catch ya soon!

In an e-mail dated 8/22/11, he wanted to tell of his experience with an Afghan fire truck. He writes, "Real quick, yes I got to drive an Afghan fire truck. It is a long story but we had to get a fire truck moved. So, I moved it. Interesting to say the least"

I used to have trouble back at home because I never knew when he would get a chance to call or e-mail. It was unsettling to carry on with household and work-related errands and risk missing the contacts that came too few and far between. I really had my faith tested and learned how to press God for prayers.

His e-mail on 7/7/11 read,

> Hey guys! Been crazy busy here. We had a thing over at (headquarters) this morning. Got my picture with the General again! ... Things are good. I am out of the wire pretty much every day going here, there, and everywhere. Days are long, but it make the time fly by. Better than sitting around and doing nothing. Getting HOT here. We are usually in the high 90's. Its not bad in the shade, but in the sun it is outta control. So,

things are good. I hope everyone is doing well and staying safe. Catch ya soon!

On 8/28/11, he just sent an e-mail titled "Soviet tank yard."

His e-mail on 9/8/11 read,

Hi guys, well, it's been a while. I thought I'd drop a note and say hi. Our op tempo is still through the roof, but we did get a day to go to the range and do some training. Got a couple of local guys a chance to fire some of our weapons as well. Things are going good and we are on the down side. 5 months and 4 days left to go. Its starting to cool down a bit here. Are daily highs are in the mid 90's and its dropping at night. We are finally getting some rain too. Things are heating up a bit here, but nothing special. Still relatively safe in the capital. No worries. I'm still doing a bunch of investigations and helping out other agencies with theirs. I am up to 105 missions now with no real let up in sight. It is a good thing because the days are flying by. Keep the emails coming, I love hearing whats going on at home. Tell everyone I said hi and I will be back before you know it.

The short e-mail, on 10/7/11 read, "Hey sweetie, I LOVE U. I am just out of control busy right now. I will try to call you in a little bit. If not I will call you tomorrow night."

In the following two e-mails in an effort to avoid unnecessary disclosure, I have used the word *local* for as a substitute for the actual location. In his e-mail on 10/9/2011, Gregory was excited to write of his recent missions assisting the locals. He writes,

Hi everyone! Well, I know I have been very quiet. I have been more busy than usual. I have an added job now. Long story short, we have an active duty Major that is here with us and he has gone on leave. So, I was asked to fill in for him while he is gone. What I am doing is the senior mentor to the Local City Police Command (LCPC) Criminal Investigation Division (CID), LCPC Counter Narcotics, and LCPC Crime Scene Services. It is a very big job and I am just trying to keep the ship afloat for him. This email and the following email are some snaps of me and the Major on patrol with the local Police CID. Not exactly the police cruiser I am use to!!!!!! It is an awesome job and I am psych'd they asked me to do it. I am having a blast! The pic is actually a bunch of us on our way to the site. This was my second day on the job! The raid was on a storage area and we recovered around $5 MILLION in stolen US equipment! I don't

know if I am going to be able to top that, but we will try. I am juggling basically 4 full time jobs on my own. Please bare with me as I will try to stay in touch! Keep the emails coming! I love hearing whats going on at home. Stay safe, Greg

Then his 10/23/11 e-mail said,

Hi guys, well it has been an awesome week. Where do I start. Well, as you know I am working with the Local National Police Criminal Investigation Division (LNP CID). A little over a month ago, we had a US Civilian employee for the Navy working on one of our camps. He had 3 local contract guards contracted to be his security. Well, long story short, they kidnapped and murdered him. Using various means we figured out that one of his guards murdered him. We (US Army CID, US Navy NCIS, and LNP

CID) interviewed all 3 and one of them confessed but would only admit his part and would not implicate anyone else. He has been in custody with the LNP since. We didn't have any evidence on the other 2 so we took their DNA samples and released them. Well, last week the DNA came back. It Identified the other 2. So, for the last week I have been working closely with the LNP CID and … other agencies to locate and track the 2 guys by several means. We located them and have been watching them for the past couple of days/nights. Well, very early yesterday morning we took them both into custody without incident. We took them to the Local City Police Headquarters where they were interviewed by NCIS an given lie detector tests (which both failed). They both stuck to their guns and would not give up their involvement in the murder even when presented with their DNA on his body (not in areas they would have normally touched him). So, once the US investigators were done with them, we turned them over to the LNP. Now, this is where the story takes a side note. I have gotten pretty close with my LNP guys, having done several Ops with them. The lead detective we have nicknamed "Charles Bronson" for several reasons. He looks alot like Charles Bronson. He has many scars which he has only shown to a few people and is a very … curt, modest, but very respectful guy. The fact that 3 of his countrymen could murder a "guest and friend" is VERY offensive to him. Mr Bronson and I have been the ones spearheading the hunt for these 2 … I spend alot of time with Mr Bronson and he always shakes my hand (the 2 hand clasp) and gives me the very respectful bow. When I gave him the 2 suspects, he not only gave me the "man hug with kiss on the cheek" he then gave me the "man hand hold" and that is how we walked down the hall!

My terp (who acts as my cultural advisor) was in shock. He told me he has NEVER seen Bronson do that with anyone, let alone an American. He now calls me "Jazzyjohn", which very loosely translates to "Jazzy, my brother". My terp tells me that Bronson now considers me family … Before I started working with the LNP, I didn't really interact with any Locals and I was sure this country was doomed. But actually working shoulder to shoulder with these guys, I now believe there is hope … There are some real patriots here that want the country to succeed and are doing the right thing. "In justice there is strength".

Time to get some sleep … Been a long week … Stay safe everyone!

Gregory sent a 10/31/11 e-mail describing the car bombing.

Guys, just a quick email because I am very busy today. I am going to give you the short version. There was a convoy hit by a massive car bomb and we lost alot of guys. They were from the transportation company on my camp and there were some civilian contractors and a couple of foreign coalition guys (Canada and England). We lost a total of 13 on the convoy and 4 local bystanders. 4 US wounded and 3 LN wounded. I don't think the 1 guy that survived from the rhino is going to make it though. He was burned pretty bad. I responded to the scene immediately after it happened and saw almost everything. For those of you that emailed that you think you saw me on the news, you did, that was me. I was heavily involved in the recoveries and I am trying to keep it together. I have seen alot of bad stuff in my life, but nothing could prepare me for what I saw and had to do. I want to be the tough guy and tell you it was nothing.

But it is not the case. I will be fine eventually, ... I have to go out today and do some more work with my Local guys. Nothing stops them, just another day ... I cant wait to come home ... Miss you all.

In an e-mail on 11/11/11, Gregory wrote his countdown. I did not know he kept countdowns for return dates. He writes, "89 days ... 89 days until I leave here and I will be on may way to hug my queen, my wife, my love ... 89 days until I get to see my doggie ... 89 days until I get to see my kitties ... I LOVE YOU!"

In an e-mail on 11/21/11, Gregory wrote, "Got up at 4 am and just got back 1115 pm. Long day but an awesome one. We went to the detention facility to interview the contractor murderer. He confessed to everything and gave us the head guy. It was a great day. Now the manhunt begins! LOVE YOU!"

In an e-mail dated 12/18/11, he shares,

Hi guys! Sooooo sorry it has been so long since I have updated. Yes, I am fine. I have had a couple of things going, keeping me on the road alot. First, my boss is on a tear and we are on the road like crazy. I had 3 investigations open. I have finally closed 2 of them and I passed off the other (took it as far as it could go). One of the investigations is under review right now and will probably go to Court Marshal. A Navy guy working at the Post Office embezzled some money. The Post Office and the Military frowns on such things. I think they want to put him in jail over this. It is going to suck for him no matter how it ends. The other thing is this. As some of you already know, I kinda hurt my wrist (non-combat related). I was carrying by "go" bag from my truck at the end of a mission to put away and

I rolled my wrist over a way it is not supposed to go. Pop and crack and no good. So, went to medical and luckily one of the Dr's is an ortho guy specializing in … wait for it … the wrist. … So he tells me that I strained and dislocated a ligament or tendon (can't remember which) and hit me with a cortizone shot … I am in an immobilization splint for another couple of weeks and then I should be good to go. I ok to still run missions, just have to change out the splint for an ace bandage and wrap it up good. The pic enclosed in this email is of me and Bobbie. He is my Bro here and this is our second deployment together (he was my roommate in Iraq). This was taken by the cliff at Bala Hissar Castle ruins that overlooks

the South East side of Kabul. The views are crazy. I am going to send 2 more emails with pics. 1 will be of the memorial service for the military guys and K-9 we lost on 29 Oct car bomb attack. The memorial was tough, but healthy. The other was me getting an award for my response to the attack. Yes, that awful thing under my nose is a mustache. Yes I hate and still have it. The short story is, I lost a bet and have to keep it till we leave. I am currently in negotiations to try to get rid of it the first week of January. Just so you know, this email has taken me about an hour to write as I can only type now. We are 38 days out until we get on a plane. I have 2 new (and very young) investigators that just arrived to replace Bobby and I. I will be spending the next couple of weeks mentoring them as I pass my cases off. In about 10 days the advance party for the Unit relieving us will be here. A week or 2 after that the main body will arrive. We will train them up and get ready to move out! We are getting short and I am keeping my head in the game. Thanks for all the emails and I will try to get back to you as I can, like I said, typing is kinda difficult and time consuming right now. But all is good! Stay safe everyone and I will see you all soon!

In an e-mail dated 12/24/11, he wrote, "Merry Christmas everyone. Stay safe and have fun. I hope Santa is good to you all. 32 days."

In an e-mail on 1/22/12, he wrote,

Sweetie, you are the best! Keep holding down the fort and I will be on my way home in 23 days. I cashed a check for $400 today. That $$ will bring me all the way home. I love you. You are doing an awesome job. Things are good here. I also mailed a big black foot locker today. You can throw it in the office if you want. It has a bunch of goodies in it. I will divide it up when I get home. You can look through it if you want. There are a bunch of T-shirts in there. And yes, some are for you.

I just cant remember the sizes right now. So, do me a favor and just leave them until I can sort through them. LOVING YOU!!!!!!! That should be it for mail you need to send to me here. ANYTHING that comes to the house for me, just hold on to. This is it sweetie. Pretty soon we will be in the teens. The advance party for the new guys is here. I am cleaning out my office right now. I can't wait to get home and give you a big ole huggies. Wrestle with the doggie, and give the kitties scratchies ... BIG HUGE kisses and hugs.

In an e-mail dated 1/16/2012, he wrote,

Well guys, we are getting short. It has been a whirl wind the last 2 weeks. The Boss has been going all over to tighten up everything before we leave. On top of that we had a couple of really high dollar items come up missing on one of our other camps. So, between everything, been pretty busy. The unit relieving us left the US THIS MORNING! It will take them a couple of days to get here and then we have to train them up. So, the countdown has really begun. The weather has been crazy. Over the last couple of days we got about a foot of snow and it has been COLD! The air quality is horrific and I have managed to get a really good head cold. Good news is my wrist is 100% and I am really happy about that. The enclosed pic is from the other day after the first really good storm we had. We were out in the middle of nowhere, Afghanistan so we took some snaps. I was pretty happy they didn't shoot at us. It has been really quiet around here as the bad guys apparently don't like to fight in the cold and snow either. Well, I gotta go start packing my stuff up and making room for the new guys. I am hoping to get

in one more update before we leave. I am looking forward to seeing you all soon. We are looking at being home 1st week of Feb, plus or minus.

Holding the Fort

While Gregory was away, he told me not to pay too much attention to what was on the news because many times it was only showing one aspect of the bigger picture. I used to especially dislike the holidays without him. I remember hearing the Christmas songs. I hated the one "I'll be home for Christmas," and I would provide my own rendition of "No, you won't." Since Gregory's suicide, I still manage to laugh with that one. He used to love the changes in the seasons and attending gatherings with his friends. For gifts, he would somehow have T-shirts from his last deployment or training to give away to his close friends. T-shirts were a big morale booster for him, and he loved giving them away. He used to stress me out by telling me not to do the holiday shopping or wrapping without him, and then he would leave it for the night before. Wherever we went with our tidings of comfort and cheer, our gifts could be readily identified as the worst wrapped ones. However, I must proudly say that we never received negative feedback from the contents of the packages. We truly were cheerful givers. The latter is probably why it was so difficult to adjust when he was deployed or away at his many trainings.

I felt like I had to try to help keep his morale up. I would keep my deployment day countdowns and send him care packages. He never asked me to do it and indeed often expressed concern that although he enjoyed sharing the goodies and treats I sent, he did not want me getting stressed out. It was weird because he worried about me and said that he was the one who had it easier. He was already at the front lines, whereas I was the one who was left in the dark and at the mercy of the media and news as it was reported. In an effort to avoid overwhelming him, I would leave big details out. For example, during the deployment after we were married, we actually bought our first home. It just so happened to have a fireplace and something called a fluke (which I later learned). Well, being raised in warmer climates, I was unfamiliar with fireplaces and was trying to save us some money on heating costs. I would start a fireplace without twisting the fluke to the open position. Oops, big mistake, but it was a huge learning experience. All the house alarms went off, and thankfully, I did know how to operate the fire extinguishers. When the smoke cleared, I could only see the whites of my eyes and those of the cats. It was like I was living in an episode of *I Love Lucy.* Well, I never disclosed that to Gregory. During our brief phone conversations (never more than three minutes or so), I had to prioritize and relay what was really important. What really mattered was hearing his voice and knowing he and his soldiers were safe and one day closer to returning home.

There were other times that I had to selectively leave Gregory uninformed. There was the time when I learned the new house he worked so hard to buy for us had termites, the time when I accidently miscalculated the garage side and swiped his pickup, and the time when I backed the riding lawn mower too far into the shed and almost took the rear wall clear off. Then there were the times when I was adjusting to the new dog he had adopted. Without telling me, Gregory had requested to adopt the retired police-trained canines. After a couple of attempts, we finally got our doggie. The dog had become accustomed to Gregory as the alpha male. So in his absence, the dog was a blessing in disguise for me. The dog and I made the local police department's morning report quite a few times because the dog would take off running down the busy street during the morning commutes. I remember one particular episode when I was walking the dog and he decided to chase a stray cat. It took me totally by surprise. I ended up getting dragged, and I lost my cell phone in the process. I was so upset and started crying because I had not heard from my Gregory for a while (like two weeks). I fell across the street from one of the new neighbors who had just moved into the neighborhood. God was looking out for me. I was not mad at the dog. The dog was being a dog. I was fighting back tears, and the kind neighbor must have heard the commotion. He saw me crying and helped me find my phone. Indeed, I had missed Gregory's call; however, I made some new friends, and I still stay in touch with them.

I imagine similar challenges that Gregory may have had to deal with while we were apart. I guess I was truly blessed that he did not have to see my weaknesses. Maybe he, too, felt the same way with me. Still, it would not have made me love him any less. I gave my best for him because I wanted to make him proud of my accomplishments. I still do in my own way. I figure his death should not be in vain. In reality, he is still living through the experiences he shared with those he served and worked with.

Being American makes you by default part of a bigger society, one that is made stronger by the many intricately different, unique, and special parts we individually play. Just like the human body, we as a society move forward because of the common movement toward advancing our species in harmony with respect toward one another's differences. Gregory was part of two important organizations—law enforcement and the military. There are many men and women who continue jointly in both roles at the same time. Regardless of the way we each earn our living, we still hold the commonality of being human, and in the end, we need each other. I cannot say I have been able to get this far alone. I owe tremendous credit to so many who stepped up to help me while Gregory was away. Perhaps that's why it has been so difficult to accept that so few have come forward since his death. I am thankful for the many people who continue to serve as sources of support, especially the fire department friends Gregory used to have. They deserve a special mention because despite their own personal stressors, I know I can still count on them to help.

Returning Home

Shortly after his returns home from training, Gregory would quickly look into returning to his roles in the home. He would take care of the vehicles, the lawn and outdoor stuff, and I would take care of the groceries and bills. He also loved returning back to his military reserves and civilian job. He loved what he did so much that it was rare to see him doing nothing. It was like keeping busy made it easier for him to take his focus off of whatever new war memories he had been made. One year on his civilian law enforcement job, Gregory earned the Mothers Against Drunk Drivers Award for making the most stops with drivers operating under the influence. What was remarkably amazing to me was that he had been away serving in the Middle East for half of that year and still managed to get the award. He always made himself available for his friends and coworkers. Whenever someone needed to call off for a family emergency, illness, or accident, Gregory was the one who would definitely step up to the plate. Whenever there was a funeral or if a unit was returning from deployment, he would volunteer for the police escort. It was okay with me because I knew I would still see him at home.

We always tried to make the most of our time together and managed to live within our financial means, so we did not take many vacations. I was just so content to be with him and have his company. I managed to make some of his favorite pastimes mine, and that also turned out to be quite rewarding as well. I learned a great deal from him, and I respected the times he needed to be with his male friends for the rough-and-tumble frolic, the movies, skeet shooting, paintball, or three-wheel rides. I loved to hear the funny stories from their outings. I remember when he got talked into joining a paintball competition. The opposing team could not stop talking about how bad they lost. The one guy said, "Out of nowhere, when you thought it was safe to move, you'd hear a faint brush move before every one of us ended up getting hit." It was awesome to hear.

Once, he and a friend who was a police man decided to buy three-wheel all-terrain vehicles. I told him, "Gregory, don't leave them outside. Someone is likely to come by and steal them."

He reassured me, "You worry too much, sweetie. Besides, they are locked and chained down." Well, when we returned from our dinner and they were both gone, I did not even say, "I told you so." But I sure was thinking it, and I sure did feel awful about the entire incident.

I remember I intentionally avoided the topic of having our own children because I did not want to pressure him. I figured being police officer and a soldier were already a lot of pressure. I surely dreamed about one day having his children. I think he sensed it because even though he avoided the topic altogether, he always volunteered us for family gatherings, babysitting, and or dog-sitting. I remember one day I came home to find a 150-pound Rottweiler drooling on the living room couch. She was adorable, and boy could that dog move. She was not the smartest canine though. She had been home for some time without realizing there were two old cats living on the upstairs floors. Gregory had volunteered us weeks before and "must have forgotten to tell me." I can still remember the sound of the dog chasing the cats down the stairs. At the bottom of the staircase, one cat veered right while the other went left, and the dog went straight through the front door, cracking it right down the middle. Well, the Jasinskas household did not sweat the small stuff. When Gregory finally noticed the crack on the front door, we were actually in the middle of redoing the windows and the doors, so it actually worked out for the better.

Yet as much as I tried to protect my protector by screening his phone calls while he tried to catch up on his sleep, I was ultimately unable. I remember about two months before his suicide, he received a phone call, and I eavesdropped on him. The caller was talking loud and fast. It sounded like Gregory had issued a speeding citation to the son an officer from the National Guard. Gregory remained calm on the phone. He responded sincerely and in a calm tone. "I can't fix the ticket. I already turned in the paperwork, and he was going way over the speed limit, driving erratically, and he was disrespectful. It doesn't matter to me that he is the son of a major. I already turned the ticket in, and even if I hadn't, I still wouldn't fix it. Wrong is wrong." I overheard the caller raising his voice and repeating something about how "his dad is a major in the National Guard" and that "if you didn't fix it, he was going to make your drill next month a really bad one."

"I still can't do anything about it," Gregory responded as the call ended. I asked if everything was okay, and as usual, Gregory preferred to keep me out of his work issues, especially during our scheduled nights together.

Well, the following month it turned out a soldier in his unit had lost an unarmed grenade launcher during one of the war exercises. What made the matter worse was that the soldier failed to disclose the mishap until three days had elapsed. As the platoon sergeant in charge of the unit, Gregory was reamed in front of his platoon. I did not hear this from Gregory. I overheard the entire incident through multiple phone calls to and from his friends. It must have been quite demoralizing. I did ask him about it, and he said, "Sweetie, it was my fault. The soldier was my responsibility. This is why I tell you to never, ever lose sight of what is issued to you, especially a weapon."

Like a true leader, Gregory deflected all the praise and took all the blame. He remained calm. I knew he was disappointed, but he told me that they had retraced their steps and eventually found the lost item. The drill exercise did not go well. That particular battle assembly also required a random last-minute inspection. I was with Gregory during receipt of the phone call from the supply sergeant who was calling to inform Gregory that his connex was missing nine issued bayonet covers. Gregory had just returned from the annual war exercise training. It was our date, and we were on our way to our favorite Japanese steak house. The supply sergeant sounded sincere in informing Gregory about his predicament. Gregory started contacting those soldiers he knew had access to the locked connex. Every caller that returned his call answered by saying, "No, Sergeant." Gregory called the supply sergeant back and told him he had not located the missing items but would continue to work on their retrieval. Well, I prayed for my husband and for the missing equipment. The missing bayonets eventually made their way back to the connex, and my Gregory did pass inspection. He definitely had a bad drill. But he had made the best of it. We enjoyed our time together and watching the flaming volcano at the restaurant where all the chefs knew my Gregory by first name. They always managed to impress.

When it rains, it pours, and they say bad events come in threes. I am not sure if there was any connection between the lost (or stolen) bayonets, the ticket issued to the major's son, and the fact that Gregory had been passed up for his due promotion. He had submitted his packet for promotion from an E-7 to an E-8, and he was denied. Under the counsel and encouragement of his mentors, he appealed. They had granted the appeal, but at the cost of some unpleasantries. Gregory had asked me if I would be available to pin him for the promotion ceremony, and I was so honored and so looking forward to it. I knew my husband had the heart of a true warrior. In the short time I have been in the military, I have had the unfortunate experience of witnessing others competing for awards, ranks, and promotions.

During my annual war exercise training, I had the opportunity to speak out about soldier suicide. We were about six days into a twenty-one-day exercise. I was under the command of an officer who had a lower rank than me but whom I respected just the same. I was ordered to go give a talk on soldier suicide, and this particular officer knew my own personal history. Well, I entered the area with my enlisted soldier at my side. We had reserved the chow hall for the lecture. As we arrived to our area, we found it was already being used. I recognized without hesitation the patch on the sleeves of the soldiers already in the middle of their lecture. I removed my cover as I entered. I am not sure if it was the amount of stripes on the chevron of the staff sergeant in front of me or the intense heat. The staff sergeant (SSGT) had the exact chevron my husband had on two years before. It was surreal. The lecturers stopped for a break, and I introduced myself to their fearless leader. The SSGT asked me to step outside. He spoke with the same calm tone my Gregory had used. He said, "Ma'am, I found this note early this morning." He disclosed that they were actually an active company that had recently returned from deployment and that they were assisting with the training. He went on to say, "I have had some recent run-ins with suicide and a surge of unfortunate suicide attempts, and I have reason to believe we have another one in this room." Well, I had been debriefed about the training exercise but knew instinctively this was for real. I calmly responded with confidence, driven by divine grace from my heavenly Father. I set my own pain aside and focused on the suicide letter the SSGT handed me. I contacted my officer in charge, following the chain of command out of respect for the exercise and the authority. I was told harshly and almost disrespectfully on my fourth attempt to forewarn my superior that we had a real-world scenario, "Just get back here, ma'am. We have the raters here."

I tuned out my superior officer keeping in mind the real-life priority. I asked the SSGT if I could take a picture of the letter and asked if he could have his soldiers sign in for us and if he would permit us to remain in his lecture. I told the SSGT that while he completed his lesson, my assistant and I would try to compare the signatures on the sign-in roster to the writing of the suicide letter. We would wait until his lecture was over, and then we would give our talk. I could share my own personal experience too. I was determined to give my best to my husband's brethren.

While the SSGT lectured, we were able to narrow down the signatures to three. I made a last-ditch effort to inform my superior officer of the case, and the officer was even harsher with me, this time demanding I return immediately after the talk was complete. To make up for the lost time, we briefly covered the required information and gave the handouts listing the contacts, and then I pulled out my wallet from my dusty, soiled uniform and took out the funeral memorial cards I had made for my husband's funeral. I made direct eye contact with each soldier as I shared the story about the handsome man pictured. I told the soldiers how two years and five days prior to our talk, the man was alive and well, patrolling the streets and loving his job as a law enforcement officer, military police officer, and National Guard reservist. They listened intently as I told them how he wore a patch just like the one they wore on their shoulders. And I pointed to the SSGT chevron and shared how his, too, looked exactly like the one worn on the uniform of the man pictured. I told them how much I missed the man because he had been my husband. He had served in the military for twenty-three years, and he had loved his life, his job, and his soldiers. I told them that despite my love for him, he chose a permanent solution for a temporary problem. And as a result, he was no longer living. I encouraged them not to make the same choice. I saw the tears well up in their eyes, and I encouraged them to please never worry alone and always ask for help. "One soldier suicide is one too many."

I rushed back to my officer in charge. I tried to share the details of what had happened, but the officer was not hearing it and instead requested the sign-in sheets for the tabulation of the data our unit was supposed to be collecting. Because of the topic and the emotions, I realized that I had erred and had not had my assistant retrieve the sign-in sheets. We had instead photographed them on our cellular phones. To avoid looking like captain obvious, I was using the photographed rosters and never collected the actual paper and because we did not have access to a copy machine, I had given the SSGT the actual sign in sheet so he could get the credit for his soldiers from the lecture. My OIC (officer in command) had a fit. The officer was not happy, not one bit. "This is why we have SOPs, ma'am. This is exactly why you have to stick to the standard operating procedure!" As the wrist slapping continued and the voice grew louder, I found myself in such a state of peace for some reason. I was able to totally tune out the unsettling tone, hostile body language, and aggressive posturing I was faced with. I stood calmly and could not help but feel the need to continue tuning it out. I was simply able to reflect on the most awesome human interaction that had just occurred in the chow hall minutes earlier with those young soldiers, and it was all worth it. They were worth it. I wondered if sharing my personal story made any difference, and I prayed deep inside for God to keep the soldiers safe, even the one yelling at me. I realized my supervisor was still quite upset. The other soldiers were watching, and it all made for quite an awkward moment. I apologized and excused myself. As I walked away, I realized that I had dropped the ball. Even though I texted her the photograph of the paper with the names and numbers of the soldiers from the lecture, I failed to retrieve the original sign-in sheet required to tabulate the date. I knew the war exercise we were engaged in was all about the numbers. I shook it off and tried to go to the happy place in my mind, but I found it quite difficult. I cried a little extra that night.

The following day the soldier who had assisted me with the lectures was reassigned to another area of the base. The noncommissioned officer who returned in his stead was approachable and listened when I discussed my account from the lecture. I asked if we could follow up on the real-world episode I had the day before. With the approval from the supervising officer, we followed up and learned thankfully that the soldier self-identified himself to his SSGT and was now receiving help under the close supervision of a chaplain. The news actually served as a positive reinforcer for me to stay in the make-believe war game without taking my supervising officer's behavior and disrespect personally. We returned with the data the supervising officer had requested and shared the real-life success story. Unfortunately, one of the raters for the exercise overheard the account and was not at all happy that he had been left out. "Why weren't we informed? This is critical information." He raised his voice at my supervising officer, who looked at me. He would not admit the truth that I had made multiple attempts to provide the information. During the heated discussion, I waited for the rater to take a breath, and in between his sentences, I said, "It was my fault, sir. I am new, really new at this soldier stuff. I am a physician, and my expertise is as a medical doctor and not yet as a soldier. It won't happen again." I looked at my supervising officer and felt the need to walk away, so I did.

I cried that night and just about every night of that annual training exercise. It was awful. We were living in tents that were either too hot (99 degrees) or too cold (38 degrees). There were twenty portable bathrooms for the 1,500 soldiers (not counting the active soldiers who were also participating in the exercise). There were twelve showerheads for both the men and the women, and only eight of them were working at a time. You had an actual three minutes of running water to shower, and if you did get some lights to work in the pitch-black shower tent, during that time you still had to wrestle with the temperature of the water. In the unlit shower tent during your allotted seven minutes, the gray water they used was freezing cold. I assume it was because it required at least three minutes before it could begin to warm up. When I went for my shower during my twelfth day or so of the exercise, the lights went out, and the water was freezing before it shut off. We did not have a place to brush our teeth, and we were not permitted to do so outside or inside of the tents. It was a dreadful experience.

I guess the one good thing that came from the war exercise was that I was able to keep my weight down. We were not permitted to do any outdoor exercise, and the tents were small and crowded. We had one warm meal a day (which usually fell in the block of time you were allowed to stand in line for the shower) and two MREs (meals ready to eat). My gastrointestinal system was not used to the MREs. I know I sound like a princess, and indeed, I joked under my breath and often told myself, "I really am a princess under all this camouflage." After the first three days of the MRE diet, I experienced awfully painful constipation. I had sweated so much during the abrupt changes in temperature and was not eager to hydrate with the cloudy, weird-tasting water that was provided. So I resorted to eating the minimal requirement. They actually forced us to pick up and carry the MREs, even if we were not going to eat them. It just made the weight we had to carry in our backpacks even heavier.

The fenced-in base we were staying at had a large water tank labeled "potable water." But there was always an unpleasant egg-like aroma, and it was either the water or the air that seemed to make the potable water unappealing. Looking back, it may have been the location. The potable water tank was right next to the gray water bladders for the shower tents and laundry tent. Regardless, it was a learning experience that brought me closer to "the force within," namely my spiritual strength and belief in God. I prayed every morning and every night to just get back home, and I was saddened by the fact that my Gregory had to endure similar nonsense for twenty-three years only to succumb to his decision of taking his own life.

During my exercise training, I witnessed firsthand the unfortunate relationship between officers and the enlisted. Some of the true colors came out from both sides in a handful of our soldiers. The little things began to just frustrate me. I could not rationalize not permitting a soldier to have a place to brush their teeth. And our unit somehow did not sign us up for the laundry service. I learned that some officers and a select few were making trips off the base to do their laundry, take warm showers, and eat real food. I turned down the invitation because I found out it was not open to everyone and that it was being kept a secret. It infuriated me. I asked the chain of command if the rumors were true, and I found out they were. It was so disappointing because I eventually caved in, but I rationalized my decision. Before the war exercise finished, my run-in with my supervising officer also did not end well. I had kept my distance until the officer called me out with a remark that struck the wrong cord in me and at the wrong time. I expressed my disagreement with the officer on a topic that just so happened to be in my area of expertise. She told me, "Perhaps you don't really belong here, Major." It was about three days before we were officially scheduled to start pulling down the tents and heading to the base. It just so happened to fall right on my birthday. As a widow turning forty-eight, I came face-to-face with my superior officer (who was a rank lower than me after all but had deployed). I actually really admired the officer. I stood there, and I realized that I could still choose to be the bigger person. I wanted to avoid saying something that could cause irreparable damage, and I did not want to risk causing harm to one of my husband's brethren. *If I say something negative*, I thought, *I will only be making a bad matter worse.* I truly was already hurting inside so much that I instead miraculously managed to respond in a calm manner (perhaps drive by the Holy Ghost), "I am not here for the rank, promotion, or recognition, and I am damn sure not here for the money. Perhaps it is you that does not belong here."

As I turned to walk away, the voice from the lower-ranking officer taunted, "There you go again, turning your back and walking away."

I calmly turned and said, "I am walking away because if I stand here, I am likely going to say something that you are not going to want to hear. So I am walking away now."

In retrospect, I really thank God I did not say more. Who was I to judge the officer? I knew I could not do the duty that person was completing with all the data collections, tabulations, and submission. The officer was otherwise exemplary. I remember I really wanted to go for a jog, a walk, or a workout just to defuse some energy. The annual training exercise we were engaged in did not permit either. It was ironic how the three things we were recommending our soldiers to do in order to avoid the suicide-related stressors were not made available to us—adequate rest, nutrition, and exercise. They say people don't care how much you know until they know how much you care. I shook off the discontent and tried really hard not to take things personal. I found myself wanting to get back home to my dog and my cats and my own shower.

The entire thing was a disappointment. Some of the soldiers (mostly officers) had been found out for leaving the base. The general in charge of the exercise therefore extended our tent time an extra day, which meant that the other units that had taken their tents down had to put them back up only to take them down the following day. I was in the chow hall for breakfast, and for the first time, I saw a higher-ranking officer eating. The officers laughed at the jokes the higher-ranking officer made, but I was seriously not happy with what was being said. It was something about how the army is run and how the decisions are made, and in between all the laughing, I was called out for a response with my opinion. I simply answered, "With twenty-two soldier suicides occurring a day, I am not sure it is running so well. Please excuse me." Then I left.

I returned home brokenhearted, and I could not help but think about how much more—exponentially more—my husband had to endure during his twenty-three years in the service. I was kind of looking forward to returning home and thought about how awesome the union would be once again with my dog and cats and how comfortable my own space would be. Prior to leaving on my scheduled exercise training, I had been asked to leave my job. That in itself is another story, but long story short, even though the US Army attorneys had looked into the matter and were able to offer me my job back, I declined. I figured I did not want to return to that kind of environment. I had once really liked it there. But now I had returned home from a challenging war exercise and at least had some downtime to look for a new job.

Life for me had changed. I did not have my husband around to bounce ideas off of. I was going home to an empty house. It was no easy road. It was not easy readjusting to my new baseline. I actually wondered if what the lower-ranking officer had said was true. Perhaps I really did not belong in the military. And now that I had no job, it was almost as if God Himself had abandoned me. And I caught myself. I wondered if this was anything like what my husband had to go through the day he reported to his work site and was pulled aside and confronted with a request for his badge. He had to relinquish his duty a police officer, the job he had worked so hard to get. I remember he did not want to tell me what really went on in the police academy, but I read about it in the newspaper and heard about it on the news. His academy class had made headlines with how they had been bullied. At one point, staff members were shoving the heads of some of the cadets in the toilet. The only way that story surfaced was because some of those cadets had to seek medical attention to rule out hepatitis. Much later he admitted to one funny story from his academy times. He said he had gotten caught sleeping in one of his police academy lectures, and the lecturer actually made him stand up in front of his class and sing. He sang Kenny Rogers's "You have to know when to fold 'em."

Even as I write this, I do not see the full picture. Law enforcement officials are so varied in their line of work. There are wildlife, federal, state, local, college, and university police along with sheriffs, departments of corrections, and air marshals. When you train all your life for a career and then it gets threatened or taken away for whatever reason, what is left for that individual? I was fortunate when I had to leave my job. I was asked to leave my job but had no immediate financial obligation, no children or dependents. But I wondered how devastating it must be to lose the lifeline of one's financial source and have nothing to fall back on. How anxiety-provoking must that be! I was blessed and provided for. And I knew my worth, and I knew that I would find another job too. My trade is always in demand. It is difficult to keep up with all the required medical and licensure requirements. Being a widow and only living on one income, it was initially quite terrifying to accept the job loss and humiliation that went with it. However, what I was put through by the police escorting off hospital property was nothing in comparison to what my husband had to go through. I was sulking later with a friend who played it down by saying something like, "Yeah, but they must have thought you were so tough to require a police escort." But I also had a sense of peace. I knew that if my husband was around, he would believe in me, and he would be able to convince me that I was going to be okay. I guess all those times I was raised homeless as a child did serve to prepare me for the worst-case scenario. I have survived much loss and lacking and still have managed by God's grace to get back on track. But what about others that lost their means to earn a living and were not able to bounce back?

I remembered the final phone call my husband made to me. He said, "Sweetie, even though I didn't do what they are saying I did, I can't be a criminal investigator if I am being criminally investigated. I don't know how to do anything else. I only know two things—how to blow things up and how to kill the bad guy."

I knew he was not listening when I pleaded with him "Please just come home, sweetie. We'll get through this. Please."

How did the minor unpleasant experience I went through compare to what my husband had to endure. I had the privilege to keep my clothes on, and no one asked me to "take off the uniform," as I imagine happened when my husband reported to work on his last shift. My husband called me that day and told me there would be two police at the front door to carry out the search warrant. I was asked to give another police officer a change of clothes for Gregory because they were retaining him, but why? They stripped my husband of his clothes. I was asked by the officer to include a pair of shoes, socks, and underwear! That meant that my husband reported to work and that they had stripped him of his boxers. Are you kidding me? Ugh. When I had the police escort me off the premises from my job, I was not even thinking about what I was losing. I was focused on what my husband had to have gone through. I wondered how awful my husband may have felt that day, what his coworkers were thinking. No one readily stood up for me when I was being escorted off the premises. But in my line of work, my former employer could not request that I leave the tools of my trade. I had the knowledge from my education within me. But with my husband, they took his badge, uniform, cruiser, weapon(s), radio, and identification, and God only knows how they justified taking his underwear. Whatever happened to innocent until proven guilty? Did it not apply to our law enforcement officials?

As I packed the last of my belongings into a black plastic trash bag, the thought of what my husband was put through almost incapacitated me. It was only then that I noticed the officer with tears welling up in his eyes. I must have been reflecting some kind of pain. I apologized to him for taking up his time. He continued to hold the door open. He spoke softly as he added, "I have to escort you completely off the property, doctor."

I held my composure, keeping the bigger picture in mind, recalling the verse that says, "The steps of a righteous man are guided by the Lord" (Psalm 37:23). I responded by calmly saying, "Sure, no problem, Officer. I understand you are doing your job, but I have to warn you. I parked kind of far."

"Does our law judge a man before it hears him and knows what he is doing?" (John 7:51). You have to pick your battles, and we all know a bulldog can take a skunk out in a fight if it has to. But is it worth the stink? My husband was not expendable, and you and I aren't either. My husband was a warrior who was trained, highly skilled, and submissive to his authority. You could wake him from a deep sleep, and he would be ready to defend the innocent from the enemy. And yet his strengths were used against him by the protocol. Indeed, "you are a slave to what controls you" (2 Peter 2:19). "He was led like a lamb to the slaughter" (Isaiah 53:7). My husband did not even resist. It is undeniably disheartening the damage we humans can do to one another.

Throughout my ordeal, I, too, have tried to avoid discourse with those who want to share their opinion on the topic. And I feel that continuing in my silence is actually assisting the enemy in our mind so he can to continue to gain ground.

I remember after 9/11, I wanted to do my part to help. I remember distinctly reading Luke 15 about the parable of the lost sheep and how a good shepherd would leave the ninety-nine to find the one that's lost. Well, I had asked God to let me help. I had made a covenant verbally so that He would let me help Him with His sheep. As I then drove away from the parking lot of the hospital grounds with the police officer in my rearview mirror, I remember distinctly my Gregory's advice, "Sweetie, never cry behind the wheel." I held my tears until I arrived home. On the way I asked God, "Why? Why?" I did not hear a response, but I remembered the statement Gregory made in one of his e-mails. I had always encouraged him, "Stay in the fight. You were made for a time such as this." He responded in one e-mail acknowledging that he full well knew the price of freedom. He said that he was part of the 1 percent. He was referring to the fact that our nation's military is made up of roughly of 1 percent of volunteers. He was proudly one of them. And I am even more proud to have served him.

The Last Stop

This page is intentionally left blank because I have not been formally made of aware of what happened on the night of the alleged incident.

The Letter

Before taking his own life, Gregory wrote some people letters. Mine is still in my Bible. I have offered to show it and read it to some of his close friends and comrades in war. I often read the letter to myself. In it, he apologizes for "resigning early." I had the privilege of seeing one of the letters he wrote to a dear friend. The following letter is one I found after his death. It appears he wrote it in the event that he lost his life while at work or away on deployment. I have recreated it here in an effort to preserve the privacy which he likely would have favored.

Well brother, if you are reading this, it means something bad has happened. I guess I should have zigged when I zagged. I know I don't have to explain it to you, because I know you understand the warrior. But please explain it to everyone else. Don't mourn my death, celebrate my life and how I lived it. I died doing my duty, my life calling. I only wanted to accomplish 3 things in my life—(1) Marine, (2) Massachusetts State Trooper, and (3) marry a good woman and have a family. Well, 2 ½ out of 3 isn't bad. In going to war, I was not looking to get killed, but I'm a soldier, have been my whole life, and unfortunately soldiers die. I hoped that the day would never come, but it has. Just know, that I was prepared for it. I guess it was just karma. I really wanted to come back from war as "the hero" not the martyr. I really wish I could be around to watch your kids grow up, go to college, join the military, or whatever, help guide them through life with you. But, I guess I will have to watch out for you guys from above. Think of it as me just doing some Recon work for you, so I can give you a good brief on what's up when you guys join me. I'm trying to be funny and keep this letter light, but as I'm writing, I'm starting to think about this, and I'm sad, hoping you never have to open this envelope. Most of all, I am going to miss Maria. I know my death will destroy her. She will try to put a front of strength on, but she will be seriously messed up inside. Please, take care of Maria and watch over her. She will need a lot of attention and guidance after she is notified and probably for a while after that. I'm asking you to be there for her. For whatever she needs. To help her make the right decisions. I know it will be hard explaining to the kids what has happened and that I will not be coming home. Just do your best to explain to them that I died doing what I love and I believe there is no more noble way to go. I guess what I am saying is I would rather go in the blaze of glory than to die elderly, sick, etc. I have tried to be a good man, do the right thing. I hope I have succeeded. I know I am just babbling, but I really don't have a thought process going here (not that I usually do), so I'm just writing whatever comes to mind. Oh, Maria will probably call you first, so I am going to enclose a list of people I want you to call to let them know. She is going to have enough on her mind, she doesn't need to be making these calls, not that you do either, but this is the hand that I dealt you, sorry. As far as arrangements, the standard drill ... Everyone, Lots of Bag Pipes too, I really loved the pipes. Also, get a hold of the Marines as well, I would like someone to be there. The Police Department will assign a liaison to Maria. Don't let them give you any crap either, lol. Whatever you need as well. And tell the Chief his ass better be there too. Anyway, after I'm looking at the grass from the underside, make sure Maria takes care of the bills. She will be getting a pretty good chunk of change from my life insurance policies. I just want her to be happy. Guide her through the big stuff. Have her pay off the house, car, school loans, etc. The big stuff. And just keep an eye on her. Eventually, she will get over my leaving. When she does, I hope she will find someone that will make her happy. Don't sabotage it, as much as I want you to, but her happiness is what I want. Please, whomever she meets, just make sure he is the right guy. You know what I am talking about … She probably will end up with another doctor and that is good, like I said, I just want her to be happy. Well brother, in closing, I hope I have been a friend to you and your family. I will miss you all very much. Help me out with the things back home as much as you can. I will be watching over you.

Your Friend, Always,
Semper Fidelis

The Eulogy

Where do I start? We want to thank you all for your presence. Gregory was a great friend to us all. He lived a life of selfless service and honor and loved it. I feel so blessed to have served alongside him as a military wife and the wife of a police officer. It was not easy but extremely rewarding. I got to eaves drop on some awesome radio and phone call conversations of acts of valor but also had to see and vicariously experience the numerous results of loss. Gregory handled the extremes with extraordinary resilience, courage, fortitude, and true grit. He was held to high standards due to his profession and personal law of ethics, and to whom much is given, much is expected. My Gregory was "Trooper Jaz, high speed."

Gregory really loved his job, the brethren, and his soldiers. He freely volunteered and didn't mind when he "got forced" to stay on another shift or go on another mission. He never complained when the job or the military asked more of him. He just gave. He gave. My Gregory daily enjoyed giving life his all. From the start of his shifts where he meticulously put together his uniform the day before to the end of his shifts where he loved "cool chillin' with the cats and the dog just to watch a few episodes of *Duck Dynasty*, Jack!" He was a lover of truth and would take bullet for anyone in harm's way. He loved catching up with his friends for coffee. And just like most cops, loved his Dunkin donuts coffee.

When we took drives together, if he took a phone call, he would answer the response of "How are you doing?" with a sincere, "I'm just living the dream, brother." And he truly meant it. He had a wide range of love for music and was the only person I knew who could in one sitting go from singing Toby Keith's "Made in America" to the "Battle Hymn of the Republic" and then Lynard Skynard and Eminem's rapping. We both knew he couldn't really sing, especially the rap, where as he drove he mumbled the first few words, singing out loud only the last few words of the stanza. His rendition of Vanilla Ice was a trip.

I always thought the neighbors were going to file a noise complaint when he mowed the lawn with his earplugs in and singing as loud as he could (*over the lawn mower*). But the neighbor's didn't. For all of you here, thank you, thank you. You all don't know how incredibly loved you made me feel, especially during all those times when Greg was away for training or deployments. He really appreciated you all for all the help you gave us, especially with putting up with our dog, Beckett, and me trespassing on your yards during the early times when the dog ran away. Greg loved his dog. He referred to him as his retired state police K-9, "The fur coated chainsaw, who would always keep momma safe." Greg loved coming home after his shifts at 2:30 a.m. just to get the wet kisses from his dog and his cats.

From the age of seventeen, Gregory already knew his short- and long-term goals. I asked him how he did it, and he told me without hesitation, "I knew I wanted three things—to become a United States Marine, be a Massachusetts State Trooper, and to marry a good woman." He got all three.

He served active duty for eight years in the US Marines. I had just graduated from medical school and met him during his transitioning to civilian life while he was working as police officer for the JPVA. If you guys are out there, please know you played a tremendously positive, empowering role in his life and career. I used to walk to the VA and see him sticking those bright orange parking violation stickers on the doctors and nurses' Jaguars and Mercedes illegally parked. And that is where my love for him grew.

With Greg, wrong was wrong, plain and simple. He played by the rules and loved it. Greg did not accept excuses. He walked his talk. And he surrounded himself with those that did the same. He was dedicated to his creed as a modern-day warrior, and his bright shining aura may have been too much for some. But Gregory used his strengths for good. He ended all of his e-mails with the saying by Edmund Burke, "The only thing necessary for evil to triumph is for good men to do nothing." He truly meant and lived it as evidenced by his personal response to 9/11, which resulted in his reenlistment into the military.

He initially went back to the marines but on his first deployment returned having felt his experience was just fighting mosquitos in Camp Lejeune. He eventually transferred to a unit that "was sure to deploy." He deployed first to Iraq and most recently to Afghanistan. Even during his time apart from me, he was always with me in spirit.

I know that I not only have lost a husband, but I feel the pain of all here who have also lost a brother, a comrade, a son, a grandson, a nephew, a neighbor, a friend. God made no mistake with our Gregory. That God who does not change has loved Gregory from the beginning and gave his parents the wisdom from conception to choose the name Gregory. That actually means "guardian." God used a lot of fine, astute, brave people to make Greg the man Greg is. And I use *is*, for Gregory will continue to be in my heart with all the awesome memories forever etched in my soul. He was refined and disciplined like no other.

Our Gregory was by God's amazing grace just right for all the accomplishments of his life. And he was *sempre fi* to the core—faithful in every way to his maker, his comrades, his family, friends, neighbors, community, and the warrior ethos.

He had great parents and grandparents that provided him with the all-American upbringing. He was truly blessed even from his early years as a Boy Scout. How could Gregory not have been as good as he was in the field of law enforcement? He was taught by the best. He learned to plan ahead and guided his soldiers to do the same without envy or concern, for he knew that God had blessings in abundance for all. He was always striving for excellence in his craft, and it came natural to him. He had a knack for detail and almost made a game of memorizing the chapter and section that applied to every stop he made and every citation he issued.

Gregory was the epitome of leadership and hard work. He was really proud of his involvement with the career paths of his soldiers. In starting this eulogy, I hit a glitch and did not know how to begin. God in His grace sent me an angel in the form of a female police officer. She was poised, professional, and appreciative of the role Gregory had played in her life. She voiced how proud she was to have worked under Gregory as one of his soldiers during her first deployment to the Middle East. It turned out her father had worked as a prosecuting attorney. He knew Greg through the numerous drunk-driving arrests Greg had often made. Well, the officer says Greg had advised her during his assignment to the military police company that she would have a better chance of becoming a cop if she deployed and had veteran status. To make a long story short, the call came out from the military police company for volunteers to deploy to Iraq. Greg spoke to the young woman's father, and as the female police officer told me, Gregory told her dad that he would be deploying and that he would keep an eye on her. The officer said with a painful yet proud but tearful smile, "He told my father he would help look out for me, and he did." That is my Gregory.

Gregory had the ability to bridge different branches of law enforcement, police departments, and ranks with such ease. I asked him how he did it. And he told me that on his first tour as a young United States Marine while guarding an embassy, shots were fired, and blood was spilled. He said he learned on the field that day that his fallen comrades, regardless of color of skin, rank, or branch of service, "They all bled red." That was my Gregory.

I was so privileged to have worked alongside my Gregory. You know he had such a positive, empowering influence in my life. I am sorry for your losses and even sorrier that I cannot mention you all by name to thank you for being here. It was your brother's time to rise. It was his season. And now we must move forward. We must carry on. We must speak the truth and never, ever give up. One of Gregory's favorite saying was "If you want something, you fight like that third monkey trying to get on to Noah's ark." This is just the beginning. I love you all, and thank you for your time.

The Final Formation

Beauty for Ashes

My Gregory will not be returning home physically. It settles me to think about his arrival in heaven and how he probably wanted to volunteer to keep an eye on all of us back here on earth. I sometimes imagine him on patrol in our neighborhood as part of his new mission—divine deployment. I see the full moon at times and imagine it is him shining his flashlight from the heavens. I have always had a good imagination. It is how I managed to get though all his deployments. I grew accustomed to counting down his 365 days of tours. I would start on day one and could not wait for day number thirty and then day sixty and ninety and 150 and so on. I knew on day 260 or so, he would be gearing up to return.

When Gregory committed suicide, I started a different countdown. Instead of "Deployment Day" in my journal, I called it "Divine Deployment Day." It has not been easy getting through this countdown. I remember Gregory's good friend would call to check up on me, and at one point I admitted to him that I figured I had made it through 150 days since Gregory's passing and was from then on going to try to just count it forward and continue seeing it as one additional day of surviving the loss. It was almost like a turning point where I started to realize that this indeed was a different countdown. My Gregory was not coming home at day 364 or 365. A still, small sense of peace made me aware that my Gregory had already made it home to heaven. I found an entry for divine deployment day #336. It reads, "I came to church and was so sad and afraid of day 365 approaching; but, I opened my Bible to 'I will deliver thee in that day saith the Lord; and thou shall not be given into the hand of the men of whom thou art afraid. For I will surely deliver thee and thou shall not fall by the sword but thy eye shall be a prey unto thee; because thou hast put thy trust on me saith the Lord' (Jeremiah 39:17)."

On divine deployment day 365, I was boarding a plane heading toward Texas to attend my basic officer leadership course. It was nothing but the grace of God that saw me through that. I actually did quite well. I qualified on the 9mm and scored a perfect three hundred on the physical fitness test. I remember being out on the firing range, and I had not handled a firearm since Gregory's suicide. The sound of the range just brought him back. I remember seeing the pop-up targets. They call them green Ivans. I knew Gregory was helping the wind. As soon as those targets went up, I shot them right back down. It was kind of comforting. I really impressed the cadre. I somehow feel despite Gregory's physical absence, he continues to be present in my life and in the lives of those he mentored, helped, and served.

Following Gregory's suicide, I was left empty. It seemed that nothing I did could make a difference. Almost like rearranging the furniture on the *Titanic* or fighting for a window seat. Nothing I did seem to make a difference. I tried to take the dog on walks in our neighborhood and would get stopped by complete strangers who were well intentioned. But I was really hurt by what was said. "I am really sorry for what he did to you." I did not know how to respond, and eventually, I just stopped taking walks. I learned to walk the dog on the treadmill and avoided going outside. I had to learn to trust again. I was raised down South, where it is customary to greet everyone with a smile and say, "Good morning." My mother taught me good manners, but eventual misperceptions from a few unkind people finally eradicated that behavior. After my husband's suicide, I had to reassess that. I wanted to be lonely by choice. I wanted it that way mostly because I needed to reground myself. I felt so empty. I eventually started slowly by giving "Good morning" salutations to complete strangers.

A lot of things in my life changed after Gregory's death. I'm sure it is the same with other major losses. The event of his suicide rocked my world in a really bad way. When the dust settled, I did not have the will to live. I did not know what my purpose in life was. It literally felt like nothing was left inside of me.

The nights seemed to be too long. I prayed and felt God had turned His ear to my cries. I could not accept that my love was gone. I battled inside my mind to stay positive and find the bright side of the tragedy. I could not. I tuned into the Trinity Broadcasting Network and Daystar channels in hopes of reigniting my faith. I could not understand why God would put me through this and through hours of cognitive restructuring, searching His Scriptures and some of His earthly messengers—Joseph Prince, Bill Winston, Kenneth and Gloria Copeland, Joel and Victoria Osteen, Rod Parsley, Creflo Dollar, Jesse DuPlantis, Brian Houston, John Hagee, T. D. Jakes, Joyce Meyers, Marlyn and Sarah Hickey, Andrew Womack, Dale C. Bronner, Charles and Andy Stanley, Cash Luna, Claudio Friedzon, Guillermo Maldonado, Gregory Dickow, Jim Reeve, Franklin Graham, Irvin Baxter, Kerry Shook, Kirt Schneider, Christine Caine, Beth Moore, Robert Morris, Samuel Rodriguez, Jentezen Franklin, Sid Roth, Bobbie Schuller, Perry Stone, Jimmy and Karen Evans, and David Jeremiah and Steven Furtick. I watched the *700 Club* and started my mental rehabilitation. I moved to a new neighborhood—one closer to the grave site that I visited daily and still visit often. I found a local church and praised God through my pain. I spent endless nights of tears, silence, and prayers asking God to give me hope again. Eventually, I realized I did not have to ask for what I had all along. It was not easy. I learned that when tough storms overtake us, we can still gain strength and emerge stronger. Seasons of drought and journeys in the valleys cannot last. I carry my pain, but now with the added reassurance that I made it through. I cannot take full credit. The strength, wisdom, and knowledge I gained helped me continue to give the suicide lectures at the assigned military battle assemblies. Even though I was still greatly pained, I came to see it as a visual exercise. When I had to speak about the suicide, I mentally unpacked my virtual backpack, and with the grace of God, I have managed to compartmentalize it.

I had a lot of help. Music helped me stay grounded, and so did some of Gregory's friends, most of whom continued to hold me at a distance. God has truly blessed me with the physical presence of many of his earthly angels. I saw God's love through multiple interactions. I knew that I had the support of Gregory's family, coworkers, comrades, and friends. From the day he took his life, they refused to leave me alone. Initially, it made me quite upset because I felt they did not trust me. But then when they also took my firearms, I kind of accepted the company simply because I felt even more unsafe without my ability to protect myself from a predator (if that makes any sense). I tried to get one of my sisters to come up and stay with me. But they each had younger children, and I did not want them to remember my Gregory in a casket. I had to reflect on that scene over and over and over to eventually convince myself that he really had died. I still believed he would be returning home.

When I had to go away for my military drills and I had to put on the camouflage uniform, it broke my heart all over again. I had to deal with so much nonsense because I came into the military as a direct commission and with a high rank. It was understandable that the lower-ranked officers were not too happy with me. They had worked for years and years, and I came in with a gold leaf. My husband had given me the quick and easy instruction, "Sweetie, you really only have to salute to those with the black leaf and the birds. Everybody else pretty much has to salute you."

I then jokingly added, "So what are you waiting for?"

I still find myself laughing sometimes simply to keep from crying. I was never one to ask for help or accept charity of any kind. I did not want to be a burden on others and risk causing further pain from Gregory's loss. At the funeral I overheard some people's comments. They meant well, but the message resounded loud and clear. "Why would he do this to her? This is going to be such a burden." I did strive to try to make my husband proud. I managed to get through the days that followed one at a time. I had the help of many good people. They know who they are, and I am so thankful for the goodness and compassion I saw.

I wanted to somehow make up for Gregory's suicide. Reaching out was especially difficult because I did not have any of Gregory's contacts. His cellular phone, I was told, was never recovered, and I knew his friends through him but did not have their contact information. Eventually, some would call me, and I went to the phone company to cancel his phone and buy back the phone number. I figured contacts would eventually call. A handful did. One called almost a full year later upon returning from a deployment to the Middle East. I remember that phone call in particular because I heard the message, "Hey, Jazz, I'm back in the States and will be in your area. Want to meet up?" I had to return the phone call to that particular military police soldier who just so happened to be a police officer in New York. Breaking the news was not easy. I heard the man sobbing on the other side of the phone and just felt so helpless. *"No, no, not Jazzy! No!"*

I had memorial rings made and mailed some of those out to his comrades. As part of my Mexican-American heritage, we mourn for a year, and in some parts of Mexico, a black band is worn on the shoulder. In an effort to avoid wearing my heart on my sleeve so to speak, for the year that followed, I wore his large black watch with his police academy ring on the watch's wristband. I also found the need to wear one of his police badges inside my waistband and the gold star pin the army had given me during the burial ceremony. I visited the grave site daily with the dog. I continued to praise God through my pain and promised that I would trust Him to see me through the ordeal. I found myself frequently repeating Isaiah 54:5, which says, "Thy Maker is thine husband." And most importantly, I have had to forgive all those who hurt my husband, whether intentionally or unintentionally, knowingly or unknowingly. I gave it to God and asked Him for that same resurrection power that raised His Son from the grave. You are reading the miraculous results of the seed that's been fertilized with the blood of all those who have left life here on earth.

I realize now that we all—as different as we are—still have so much in common. We all struggle with the usual steps following loss, perhaps riddled with denial, blame, guilt, anger, and eventual acceptance. I may have wallowed in too much gloom, self-doubt, and shame. But the truth for me is centered around knowing my value as a child of the Most High. The realization of the latter has helped me understand that we are all valuable and needed, myself included. I do not think I have been the only one with survivor's guilt after the suicide of a close loved one. But looking back, I think society has thrusted us into a vortex of overstimulation from social media and the Internet, somehow desensitizing us when we fall short of meeting those intense and unrealistic expectations. I know that some professions are associated with added responsibilities, especially those involving service to the public. Yet it seems we have lost sight of the reality that despite all our society's advances, we are still human. As my husband would say, "We all bleed red." It just seems that society has set us up to fulfill unrealistic expectations of perfection.

It is as if we have overlooked the most valuable resource on earth, its human inhabitants. Technology has exponentially multiplied, and we have a false sense that everyone is dispensable and expendable. This cannot be any further from the truth. Our current computerized culture has misled us to easily discard outdated electronics, and we have erroneously transferred that to our own humanness. We are individually unique and made to fulfill special roles. Yet the fast-paced, dog-eat-dog ladder of competition and success appears to have us convinced that there is only one spot for the top dog. And that in itself is an excellent motivator to continue advancing as a society. But who says there is only room for one? The sun shines on us all, and in the end, we do need one another. No man is an island.

Following Gregory's suicide, it took some time for me to get my strength back. I still do not think I am at the baseline I was before his death. I had to fight negative, self-defeating thoughts and convince myself to just stay in the fight of life. Just putting one foot in front of the other was challenging. I hated waking up alone. I hated to see the phone because I knew it would not be ringing to connect me to him. It was awful to have to live through the experience. I went from being a proud wife to being a shamed widow. It was much worse for him, I am sure, or at least that is what I gathered from the tone of the letters he left behind. Ironically, we had discussed the topic multiple times. He used to say that he wanted to have "a hero's death." We watched war movies about heroic acts of courage and valor, and he would always say he would put up a fight and make every effort to come home from a battle or tour of duty alive. He told me once that he would not be afraid to meet death but that he would be sad for the people he had to leave behind. I used to change the subject when watching those kinds of movies resulted in that kind of talk. I wanted to believe we would be together forever. I liked believing we were going to grow old together and retire to live in Montana or another red state.

Identifying as his wife was enough for me, and I was content to stay in the background and on the sidelines as his biggest fan. It did not matter to me what the pressures of my career threw at me because I had a husband at home to cheer on. I supported his every tour, his every detail, and his every deployment. I used to tell him, "We only have one life to live, and I do not want to stand in the way of you getting where you want to go." I meant it. What made him happy for the most part made me happy because I was an expert at conceptualizing my perception of the situation. I did not challenge irrelevant things. I did not have to have the last word in a discussion. We respected each other and had many issues we agreed to disagree about. In the end, I did not have to be right. I just wanted to love him unconditionally just like my heavenly Father loved me. Gregory helped me with my life goals, and I helped him with his. We were an awesome team. He was an amazing husband—tough yet tender. Before I met him, I struggled with being alone, and I always knew I would be married someday. He told me once, "Sweetie, I want to be everything you ever want in a man." He was. I guess that is why it has been so difficult for me to get the wind back in my wings.

You see, when my late husband chose to take his own life, he took part of me with him. I was initially left empty and without a mission. During the thirteen years of our relationship, I made him my mission. I loved him like I thought God wanted me to love. I can proudly say that my husband never had to worry about me nagging him because I learned early on that I could change my own way of thinking and deal more effectively with whatever issues arose. I did not have to have the last word because I saw our union as one. If he hurt, I hurt. If he won, I won. Perhaps I am guilty of giving him the credit of "putting wind beneath my broken wings and helping me fly." Only after his absence did I learn that God was in control all along. It was God who made sure our paths crossed. Ultimately, He knew how that chapter in my life would end, beginning yet another season that I am still trying to figure out.

I for one have been guilty of judging too abruptly, especially judging myself. After Gregory's suicide, I felt isolated, ashamed, and without value. My mission had ended in failure. I felt that others were keeping their distance from me because of their disappointment with him and with me. Regardless, I could not judge his act or hold it against him. I felt like people were not calling or offering help because they were blaming me. I knew I had failed in some way. I failed reaching out to others. I failed accepting help. But in retrospect, I was projecting my disappointment onto others. I saw people in marriages making mountains out of molehills, and I had to fight within me to avoid voicing my opinion. I thought, *How could they take each other for granted like that?* I would return home to my aloneness (if that is even a word). And I would ask God, "How can they hurt each other? Don't they know they have what so many do not?" I remembered in my own years of counseling and introspection how I was told that it was not good to compare ourselves to others because we are all at different levels of coping. So despite my frustration and sorrow around the loss of my husband, I began to choose instead to let go of those thoughts.

It almost became comical to me during my first attempts at reentering the social scene. I felt like a recluse under a microscope. I had forgotten how to apply makeup, and even though I was never a slave to fashion, I could not even find the will to try to look good. When I attempted to coach myself and challenge the negative thoughts, I felt like I was taking my little fist to a gun fight. At first, I accepted dinner invitations associated with charity events. And initially, I was bitter that I had no one to sit next to. I really did not appreciate the thought of being a burden. And I loathed even more the thought of being the third wheel. *Ugh, I can't win*, I thought. I found it really difficult to start conversations.

At one point I actually just proposed to one kind gentleman. He was single and in the same line of work as my husband. Out of the blue, he just reached out to offer his help, and I was still in a fog and in shock from my loss. I am so glad he declined my marriage proposal. I eventually realized I could not love others if I did not love myself. I was blaming myself. I had accepted God's forgiveness, but I had not forgiven myself. How was I supposed to give a love I did not give myself? I felt like everyone knew my circumstance, and I did not want anyone feeling sorry for me. I recall going to one dinner and being asked about my husband. I could not lie. I make an awful liar. I twitch when I lie, and that would always give me away with Gregory. It was quite silly, but I had to learn to be selective about my disclosure. I think it had a lot to do with the basic human need of wanting to belong. I was going to be okay. I just needed to start believing in myself again.

When I overheard couples bickering over silly things, it just made me even more upset. I was thankful that no one asked me my opinion and that I had learned not to give it. It was so painful to see couples that weren't appreciating the very breath they were breathing. I felt so vulnerable. With God's grace, I eventually managed to shrug off the discomfort. I set aside twenty minutes a day for my own pity party. It helped me stay true to the pain I had to process and yet kept me free to attempt to start over.

I eventually adjusted, and I often went to my mental happy place. I would remember similar disagreements between me and my Gregory as a couple. I recalled how Gregory would get on my nerves when he left his shorts or socks on the living room floor. I used to get so frustrated until one day I came home and found Gregory picking up his shorts and socks. The dog had gotten into the habit of carrying Gregory's stuff to his favorite spot on the floor. The dog had gotten into the habit of making a nest with Gregory's clothes. Funny how life throws those little mysteries at you. I gained a lot of comfort and therapeutic counsel from my four-legged friend.

Following Gregory's suicide, our dog almost died. He literally shut down. He stopped eating and would not play ball or leave his crate. It was awfully unsettling. He went from 115 to eighty-three pounds. Looking back, I realized it was largely my fault. I took him to the veterinarian, and after an extensive workup, nothing was found. The dog literally had a full-body MRI scan, lumbar puncture, cardiac echo, and costly blood tests. Every body organ was scoped and probed. They found nothing but a low vitamin B-12 and a mildly elevated lyme titer.

I had lost my bounce, and I had made it a habit of crying myself to sleep often and in front of the dog. I, too, had lost weight and interests, and now I was losing my dog. I prayed for him. I told God, "I will trust You with or without my husband and with or without my dog. Take him as well, if You need him up there. I will trust You." I eventually decided to redirect my vision and outlook. I had misperceived that in order to be of value to society, I needed my identity as a wife. In some bizarre way, I had morphed to accept—like Gregory did—that my life was over. And really it was only beginning. On the date that would have been our wedding anniversary, instead of staying home and crying, I went flying. I took my first flight lesson. It was nothing short of awesome, outstanding, and unforgettable. When the door of the plane's cabin flew open on takeoff and my certified flight instructor had to reach over and close it, for the first time in a long time, I felt my heart beat again. Up until that moment, I had been going on automatic pilot, just putting one foot in front of the other without much thought or sensation. But when we took flight and I saw the clouds and the hawk that flew by us, I was all in. A childhood memory came to mind. I was about three years old and out in the tomato fields. There were wooden crates for stacking the tomatoes before they were sent to the packing house. Well, to pass time, I used to stack two crates in a "T" formation. I used to sit in the lower one and position the second one horizontally. I used to imagine I was flying an airplane, and I would pass the hours in my makeshift cockpit. I used to dream of flying. Fast-forward forty something years later, and there I was, flying for real. What an incredibly uplifting experience. It made the pain I had been carrying somewhat less of a load.

My dog also soon thereafter recovered from absolutely nothing other than what sounded like the human equivalent of an acute reaction of grief. We are both still on the mend. I am slowly learning to laugh again, and my doggie is once again able to chase balls, squirrels, rustling leaves, and pretty much anything that moves. As painful as life continues to be, I catch myself getting sad and have to stop. Then by the grace of God, I will just remember a silly joke and let myself laugh out loud. I actually do not remember many of the ones Gregory told me. But, I have learned some new ones since his suicide. The one that comes to mind often is this: "What do you do when you are riding a wild stallion with a giraffe on your left and a roaring lion behind you? Get off the carousel."

I am kind of embarrassed to admit that I have had to learn to laugh again, and that is so sad but so true. To this day, I am not at all proud to admit that I still have to fight back tears when I see a Granny Smith apple or other triggers that remind me of my fallen hero. The Granny Smith apples were his favorite. They are too tart for me, but he used to down half in one bite. I can eat a Granny Smith apple if it has at least three thick layers of caramel and coconut. The dog and I still love to share the Washington red apples. He still tests the boundaries with my cats, and it just boggles my mind how my outlook on life has changed. I used to look forward to serving Gregory his dinner. How crazy is that? He was so easy to love. His dinner requests were so simple that even I could not mess them up. The five days a week he ate dinner at home it was macaroni and cheese (from the box) or spaghetti and sauce. He did not even ask for homemade meatballs. He liked hot dogs and canned baked beans, tacos, and pizza. We would order pizza delivery once a week and go out for dinner once a month.

When Gregory died, I felt that love had left. I failed to realize my worth. The culture we live in can be so cruel. I stopped fighting and gave in to accepting and settling into the role of the widow. I had been his wife. I had only identified as his wife. But after Gregory's death, I still carry his name. I did not die with Gregory, or did I? I continued weeping over his death and then realized that if he was in heaven, he was much better off than me. My dream of living with him died, but now I had to choose to live again and to dream another dream. The realization that life goes on was a painful truth.

I do not want to compare my trauma to that suffered by anyone else because I feel God gives each of us grace to endure the trials we face. But the fact that I witnessed others move forward with their lives despite their losses made me question my own intentions and motives. I realized my real worth did not come from the one that gave me his last name. Although I bear it proudly, I am hopeful that with Gregory's passing, I can eventually move forward. I was looking at his passing from the bottom up rather than from the top down.

Gregory did his time here on earth. He perhaps perceived having accomplished the missions he set for himself. In his lifetime he saw more human atrocity than most. Who was I to judge his final decision? I was left out of that final decision, and that was an epic disappointment. In the end, I trusted him and still do. He told me once that he was not afraid to die but that he was afraid for those he would have to leave behind. I know the decision he made to end his life here on earth was not an easy one. Indeed to most, it was probably seen as "the coward's way out." But I assure you that Gregory was no coward. In my mind, he was and will always be a mighty man of valor. Society let him down. His job let him down, and I let him down. Earth's loss of a great warrior was heaven's gain. We as a society need to revisit the way we treat one another, especially those who protect us from harm and the many enemies of the United States. This is not just my fight. This is our fight, the fight for our children's future, and the preservation of generations to come will pay the price if we continue to ignore suicides, especially among those individuals at higher risk. If we as a society can continue to turn away and sweep under the rug the tragedies the families of our nation's defenders are facing, we will not be able to shed light on this unpleasant topic. Ignoring the problem will not make it go away.

We have to slow down and acknowledge the intricate, individual value each human brings to the table. I cannot do anything to bring Gregory back. Gregory's death by suicide despite his countless acts of valor prior to it did not make him a hero. And nothing I do at this point can bring him back. Yet I do know his death served a much greater purpose. If anything, it has fueled my passion to serve his people, his soldiers, and his comrades.

Gregory used to joke around and say that he was my case study. When I accompanied him to his police or military gatherings, his friends would jokingly comment on his uncanny ability to just stand out. He was so secure in his identity as a civil servant, but when his integrity and reputation were threatened with slander, it must have taken even him by surprise. How could the people he so readily protected turn on him? I still do not believe they would willingly harm him. They did not see his suicide coming. They say we cannot prevent what we cannot predict. It seems they did not do anything intentionally to hurt him.

He just refused to take the walk of shame in front of the media and the scandals that would surely follow. He told me on one of his last phone calls, "Sweetie, even after the year is over and I get found not guilty, I will still always be that guy."

On the morning after his death, I was in a fog. My world had been shattered, but the reality of Gregory's suicide still had not set in. I honestly thought it was some kind of misunderstanding or nightmare. I had the dog on the leash and was staring at the ground as I walked up the short paved driveway. I saw patent leather pumps and a yellow pencil skirt. It was the woman from our morning news with a microphone aimed at my face. I stopped in my tracks almost in shock as she said, "Would you like to make a statement?"

In my peripheral vision, I saw a giant microphone on a stick above the bushes. I could not believe it. I said calmly, "No." The reporter repeated her question, and the dog must have sensed my change in demeanor. I looked at the woman, "Yes, I can't hold this dog. You need to leave." The dog stood up on his hind legs and gave an awfully aggressive growl. "That a boy. That's a good boy," I encouraged him as the news van pulled away.

The days that followed were unimaginably uncomfortable. The two police friends Gregory had would not leave me alone. They shared shifts as one came and went. I knew it was difficult for them and their families. I felt awful about my own personal loss and even more awful that his friends now were likely worrying about me succumbing to the same fate. I willingly gave up my firearm to help them. Even though I did not have the ability to pull the trigger on myself, I knew I would not be able to convince them, especially given the fact that their own close friend had likely given them the same false reassurance. I somehow felt the need to stay in the fight of life. Even at my lowest point, I somehow believed God would help me make something good as a result of Gregory's death. As impossible as it seemed, I just wanted to turn back the clock. I pleaded and begged God to give me some answers. He didn't. I guess that is what real faith is all about. I so wished that I could make something good come out of the tragedy, but I felt my efforts would be futile. My husband had taken his own life. In an effort to carry my own weight and relieve my husband's friends, I made some phone calls to my family. I opted against having my sisters or brothers come up to be with me because they all had younger children and they knew my Gregory as a hero. I was already down and was unable to explain to their kids how my husband, who had been so full of life, healthy, and free from any sickness, cancers, or diseases, freely chose to take his own life. I remembered a girlfriend I knew would be available. God sent an angel in the form of my girlfriend. She hopped on the first train and kept me company for the few weeks that followed. Only then was I able to relieve the two policemen, and that was only after they picked her up for me and brought her home. Thank God for friends. She helped me with everything, and looking back, I felt so bad for her because I did nothing but weep in her presence.

It was nothing but God's grace that got me through that ordeal, especially that first week. In an effort to avoid scandalous stories from surfacing, I asked for help in burying my husband as soon as possible. He took his life on a Monday, and his military drill was for that weekend. It was all a blur. Somehow things came together thanks to Gregory's friends. I ended up feeling physically ill. I had to go to my primary care doctor for some excruciating pain in my ears. It turns out I perforated both eardrums from grinding my teeth too hard during my sleep. The doctor had kindly offered me some antibiotics and sedatives to get by. I declined the sedatives. I thought that avoiding the pain now would drag it out longer. Consider the times when you break a bone. If you take the analgesics, it slows down the healing process. I just did not want to make a bad thing worse, and I wanted to be strong. I wanted to feel all the pain as if that in itself could earn me passage out of my misery. Well, it did not. Every day got worse before it got better. And my friend eventually had to return to her own life. And I turned to the life I had left. I went back to work and felt like everyone was looking at me.

I managed to hold it together at work. I did not make any mistakes. On the contrary, I kind of appreciated having something to keep me busy and distracted. One kind coworker innocently attempted to confront me. "Dr. J, I don't know what to say. You used to come in here and just brag about your husband and your dog, and now I just don't know what to say."

I had been firm at my workplace before my husband's suicide regarding certain issues that were standard of care and not within my area of training. I managed to hold my ground and continued to provide exceptional care in my areas of expertise, namely general psychiatry, child/adolescent, and geriatric psychiatry. I had returned from my annual military training, where I also miraculously excelled. On the range I was one of the officers who actually qualified on the M9. I imagined God and Gregory looking down and helping me because every time the target popped up, I managed to pop him right back down. And on the physical fitness testing, I scored a perfect three hundred. However, upon my return to work, I heard it through the grapevine that the hospital's CEO was going to try to enforce his new protocol, and if I continued to decline, he was going to make it look like I needed to go. I received the intel from a reliable source. So I gave my thirty-day notice. The CEO had already terminated one of my good colleagues whom I respected and admired dearly. He actually had her banned from the hospital. Everyone who knew the doctor knew the reason was bogus. Ever since that incident, I kind of lost the CEO's trust. The CEO and the medical director called me into a meeting and actually tried to make it look like I was depressed. They used my weight loss as a sign to suggest that I was clinically depressed. They tried to bully me into believing that my stand in refusing to prescribe certain medications was also unsatisfactory. With a coy, unsettling smile, the CEO gave me a letter. It turned out he had some kind of legal background and caught me in a loophole. Since my month away at the military training on top of the three weeks I took off for Gregory's suicide fell in between the yearly contract renewal, he said I would have to work the thirty days without pay. I took the news in stride. Even though I felt hurt, betrayed, and disappointed, I settled in my heart and mind that my God was still in full control. That final month at that hospital was quite a challenge. But by the grace of God, I got through it.

My husband's suicide had left me and those closest to him quite stunned. Gregory was not one to have shown any signs of premeditating his own death. Yet even in his darkest hour, he did not choose to take others down with him. For the funeral, I had to decide what uniform to bury him in. I was not able to bury him in his civilian uniform, even though that was what he stated as his preference. I learned that much from the suicide letter he wrote and mailed me. He took his life on a Monday, and I did not get the letter until the Wednesday. The decision had already been made. I did not want to bury him in his National Guard uniform. He had the uniform already prepared for the upcoming military police ball. Like all major issues in my life, I prayed about what I would bury him in. The thought came to mind to bury him in his US Marine Corps uniform. The police friends and a soldier from the National Guard helped me. It just so happened that our neighborhood dry cleaners was owned by a National Guard reservist infantryman. That particular individual was another heaven-sent angel in the form of a human. I will call him Mikey. Mikey had always been ready to assist my husband and me with uniform emergencies. And he delivered. It is sad to say that unfortunately there were a slew of suicides following my husbands, and Mikey became known as the guy who could deliver in preparing the uniforms. I still keep in touch with Mikey. He does not know it, but he is one of my modern-day heroes. He decided not to reenlist when his military contract came up for renewal. I knew he had had reservations, but I was glad to see that he was able to get what he needed from the military, give his best, and move on.

My husband chose a different option. My husband turned his own gun on himself. And to all my readers who are against guns, please don't write me to share your hate for firearms. I for one feel proud to be a part of a country that still respects my second amendment right. "A well-regulated Militia, being necessary to the security of a free State, the right of the people to keep and bear Arms, shall not be infringed." I often reflect on the 9/11 attacks. The perpetrators on the two planes that crashed into the World Trade Center were said to have used box

cutters. Regardless of all the hate, anger, and evil that exists, I still believe in the good in all of us. Gregory did not have to die. Neither did the others who have gone before him or those who will unfortunately make the choice he made. The fact that he chose a gun is not the issue. The underlying issue is much deeper. We make good choices by making right decisions. Society let him down, and with the diffusion of responsibility as is often seen when large groups are involved, no one can really take responsibility. In the end, no one but Gregory made the choice. Yet we can each be part of the problem or part of the solution. When the last second here on earth came for my Gregory, all the rank, ribbons, awards, and recognition made no difference. His blood ran just as red as those who had died before him. Gregory's passing was for a higher purpose. We have to look out for one another. The fact that you chose to pick up this book and learn more is proof that there is hope.

I for one am praying over everyone who reads this book. It is now my mission in life to continue interceding for the families of those who have died and those who have to face the choice. My hope is that you choose to live. Like the psalm says, "I shall not die but live" (Psalm 118:17). I wish my book could have a happy ending. But the truth in life does sometimes cause pain. Every generation can serve to assist the one that follows us, and just maybe we can as a society stop to learn and grow.

I am foolish and naïve to still believe that there truly is beauty in these ashes. 9/11 was a call to arms to every American. We all answered the call differently. Indeed, some still continue in denial that we are even at war. Ignoring the problem is not going to make it go away. I like to believe that even the evil brought on by our adversaries can help us if we learn the experience. We have to do something. This book was my effort to at least raise awareness. If we keep doing what we are doing, we are going to keep getting what we are getting. And one precious life lost is one too many. The latter is true regardless of creed, trade, skin color, socioeconomic status, or spiritual belief. The words of a wise man still ring true, "The enemy is out to steal, kill, and destroy." We can turn the tide. We can regain ground. I do not have all the answers, but I do know this. We can make a positive difference one kind word at a time. As Mother Theresa said, "I can't do what you can do. You can't do what I can do, but together we can do great things."

Suicide leaves many unanswered questions. Denial of the topic altogether does no one any favors. As painful as this all is, we have to forgive completely, and we have to commit to making a change. My husband's suicide left many people angry. But it was not like the truly cowardice moves of the jihadist who have a reckless disregard for the innocent lives they target. Sure, my husband's act left those around them in emotional pain. But in the end, he was left alone, and the media was standing ready to scandalize and assault a man not yet even charged.

The suicides occurring do not appear to imply the request for favors but simply a return to the respect for human kind we used to have. With all due respect to our nation's current leaders, denying or ignoring the issue of suicide is no longer appropriate. This country was founded on checks and balances. And it seems the checking must start within us, especially with the words we use.

I for one refuse to go back to my period of mourning. I had thirteen good years with a man God trusted me to love and care for. I will not give up on life. I will not give up on love. Although I have grown accustomed to the uncomfortable pain that is within me, I will continue to make every attempt to combat it by choosing daily to make this place better and helping whoever I can, even if it is just giving an encouraging word or a smile. I encourage you the reader to do the same. I found carrying heavy burdens of unforgiveness toward others or circumstances only served to decrease lift and increase drag. I had to forgive completely.

On Memorial Day of 2015, I went to the grave site and saws two soldiers there. They were sitting at the foot marker, and they recognized

me. They did not realize the bench was part of Gregory's grave site. I had designed a bench with cross sabers as the back. His photo is etched on the back. I showed them the headstone, and we all kind of laughed. For about two years, the tombstone had not had Gregory's first name. It just had his middle name. One of the soldiers thanked me for the eulogy. He actually said that Gregory was the ninth suicide from that unit in that year. The soldier said he was planning on being the tenth,

but something in what I said had helped him get help. I cannot describe how that felt. I made a positive difference. I had taken a risk and made a difference. I thanked the soldiers and invited them to my home for a Memorial Day service in honor of my husband. I had T-shirts made for the special occasion.

Despite my efforts, only three soldiers showed up. One was actually attending a ruck march in honor of the fallen soldiers. Maybe the fact that no one else showed was for the better. I was a hot mess. I managed to stress myself out. But some good did come out of it. I met a couple of really good friends from Project New Hope. And I helped support a local T-shirt business owned by one of the firefighters. Gregory was always into his T-shirts, so I had memorial T-shirts made and just gave them to the few soldiers who did show up. In retrospect, I guess I was kind of relieved because I was not sure how to celebrate someone I was still mourning. I looked back over the time since Gregory's passing and realized I still had no answers. I had a lot more questions but still no answers.

During one of my drill weekends, I was sitting through yet another suicide lecture and found myself so sad. I remembered Gregory and how he used to love driving and singing. I so enjoyed our drives together. He had a list of favorite tunes he played. He loved singing along to Toby Keith. I especially enjoyed listening to him sing "American Soldier". Believe it or not, he actually even sang along to Nat King Cole's "What a Wonderful World". We loved listening to Whitney Houston's "I'll Always Love You". I struggled to fight back tears during the lecture, and I attempted to distract myself by looking at the text I had received on my cell phone. The really cool thing was the place we met had such poor cellular reception, and it is highly unlikely to get good reception. But I saw that someone had posted a photo of my sweetie on the Run for Fallen Heroes board, and it just lifted my spirits.

You see, I really feel everything happens for a reason. I do not want the blood spilled by my husband and all those who have died because of similar circumstance to go to waste. No one is expendable—*no one*. We all carry an innate unique quality and priceless value. His death was for a higher purpose. Let us learn from this and make changes to avoid more deaths to suicide. Even if we act to save one life, we will have won.

Since Gregory's suicide, many of his friends and coworkers have kept their distance for whatever reasons, and that is okay by me. They continue in my prayers, and I know with Gregory's death, they, too, were at a loss. We all grieve differently. Many of his coworkers and comrades have remained in touch. Life goes on. And despite their lives moving on, I know if I need help, they are a phone call away. For example, one of Gregory's friends helped me with the dog when I had to go away for my military training. Despite the unpleasant contact between my dog and his, we eventually came through, and from that unfortunate experience at the kennel, I was introduced to an amazing person who specialized in ... German shepherds. The woman, Shari Ann Murphy, is a saint. She and her husband helped my dog, and I regain our footing in so many ways. She has always come through for me and my doggie. She watches my four-legged friend whenever I have to go away for my military leaves and miraculously taught him how to readjust to my husband's absence. I tried to take my dog to normal kennels, but they'd take one look at him and deny us access. I guess German shepherds do not play well with other dogs. I still do not know how she did it.

Since Gregory's suicide I have made efforts to stay in contact with his friends because I know how much Gregory loved them. I had some memorial rings made that I mailed to those I had addresses for.

When I wanted to grow weak, I would remind myself of 2 Samuel 22:42, which reads, "God has armed me with strength for the battle." One of Gregory's friends actually had a memorial carbine made in his honor. I received the first one and was so honored that my sweetie had been remembered like that. I know he would have loved to see it.

My hope is that in successfully staying in my fight for life, I may be a source of encouragement for others who have had to go through a similar tragedy. I do still think that something good can result from this. Hope is rising, if we choose to make it so. Perhaps in a way my hero perceived he had completed his life mission. If that is the case, then maybe we just have to keep dreaming and moving forward in life by setting additional goals.

If I let myself, I can get stuck in sulking over his loss and just fuel that feeling of ineffective negativity. In all honesty, I do at times feel like society used my husband for his skills and then just abandoned him. When the image of an organization is at stake, it does seem like the media chooses to side with the authority figure in the highest position of power. Often the choice appears to be one of appeasement. Yet is it not an irony that that which we fear most is what we neglect? Gregory's suicide was not predictable a week before. He left no signs. He was a master at camouflage. His training as a man of war enabled him to mask his external and internal signals, deterring detection in the end even from aid. My husband's strongest assets included integrity, reliability, loyalty, and acceptance. But walking in his boots, can we be the judges? After all, even those who were supposed to protect him left him with no viable choice to avoid the unproven onslaught of slander and shame.

I know this is not just about me. There are so many families that have been negatively affected by the numerous suicides. Among military and law enforcement, the growing rates are disheartening. It is true that our safety is our own responsibility. It is not the responsibility of the police or the military to protect us. However, without their presence, we run the risk of going back to how it was with even more crime, violence, gangs, and danger. I for one refuse to live in fear. I want to encourage whoever reads this to stay positive and appreciate those who put their lives on the line for ours.

It is not a lie that bad things happen even to good people. But it is how we respond to the circumstances that can make or break us. I received a text from a friend more than two years after the suicide. He texted, "Thinking about you. Hope you are doing well."

I responded the following day, "Thanks. I'm living in faith, knowing God is in control. I sure do miss my love, but what can I do? If a dream dies, I can't die with it." I do reflect back on that dreaded day when I saw my love drive away. I so wish I would have for once just resisted submitting to his authority as my husband. I catch myself falling into those "would have," "should have," "could have" traps and redirect myself by saying, "*I will not should on myself today.*" I chose to let a day go by between receipt of the text and my response mostly because I was not ready. Every interaction and decision we make affects not just ourselves but those around us. It is amazing to me how the memory of a person is attached to a string of unique recollections. I had made a lot of friends through my husband—good people, really good people. I wished the friend who texted me happy holidays and reassured him as I often do, "You and your family continue in my prayers." They do, and now I figure my mission is a lifelong continued prayer for them and whoever is reading, has read, or will read this book. I now add you, the reader, to my prayer list.

I pray different prayers but mostly revert to a prayer an old friend taught me from the first chapter in the book of Colossians. When Gregory was alive, I would switch it up with my favorite prayer originally by Oswald Chambers in his book *My Utmost for the Highest*. Oswald Chambers said he initially learned it from one of Austria's prime ministers. I have changed it so much over the past couple of decades that I am sincerely not sure how much still belongs to the original, but it goes something like this.

Lord, God Almighty, my Creator and heavenly Father, as the sun from heaven shines down and renews our minds, so too does the sunshine of your great Spirit warm our hearts and our minds, renewing us by the power of Your wondrous grace. I am now emptying from my mind every thought memory and idea that is not in harmony with Your goodness. I hereby drop from consciousness every selfish, evil, and unworthy thought. I let go of all uncharitable attitudes, every fear and vestige of ill will and resentment. As our minds are now cleared of every unhealthy thought, You are now filling them with thoughts of goodness, love, faith, wisdom, peace, understanding, counsel, courage, knowledge, piety, fear of the Lord, chastity, joy, patience, kindness, generosity, gentleness, self-control, and the ability to solve any problem that lies before us. Thank You, dear Lord, for I can feel at this moment Your freshening and renewing power, and it feels wonderfully good. Thank You for our wonderful bodies, which only You can make, for our knowledge and wisdom-filled brains, for our strong hearts, our good stomachs, our healthy livers, our keen eyes, our sensitive ears, our fully functioning cardiac, respiratory, immunologic, musculoskeletal, dermatologic, reproductive, genitourinary, and central nervous systems. All parts of our body are working at Your prime state. Thank You for that immortal part of us, our souls, which I place once again in Your keeping so You can continually fill them with the beauty and joy of Your spiritual light. Thank You for Your grace, love, and forgiveness and for the peace of mind and wisdom You are giving us every day all the way in Jesus's name. Amen.

The days that followed Gregory's death were difficult. For the months that followed and intermittently since, I often find myself automatically still naming him before I start my prayers. It is a long road ahead, but there is hope. My prayer for you is that you too move forward in victory, knowing that tough times are going to continue, but you can stand stronger as a result. Reach out. Do not isolate. Remember, you are more than the temporary problem you are facing. If you lost a loved one, you will be able to love again. If I did it, anybody can. Believe in yourself, and know you are equipped to fully handle whatever problem comes your way. You will rise above the challenge. You do matter. You were uniquely made. The world needs you, and I need you to help me keep moving forward.

I heard it said that since the 9/11 controversy, the number of war-related deaths in the battlefield are less than a third the amount when compared to the suicides of our nation's soldiers and veterans during that same time period. When I googled US Marine Corps suicide rates, I read that during the Iraq and Afghanistan wars, more marines have committed suicide than ever before. I started this book out by saying that I am not pointing the finger at anyone. And I do believe everything has a season, and given that an election is around the corner, I would guess this would be an excellent platform for our country's leaders to address. Despite the discrepancy with the actual rate of suicide—some statistics say one a day, and others say twenty-two—the truth is that one is one too many. Suicide is not just taking the lives of our soldiers and law enforcement officers. It is also an epidemic among our adolescents and young adults involved in neither of those areas.

In Spanish, there is a saying, *"Todo lo que brilla no es de oro."* (That saying translated reads, "All that glitters is not gold.") In a sense, Gregory was at the top of his game, and no one expected him to take his own life. I did not even see it coming. He was especially happy before his last deployment. We cannot just assume that suicide is only taking the lives of those with financial problems or drug-related addictions or losses. Suicide is not a respecter of persons. It can affect anyone from any walk of life. Ignoring the problem does not mean it will go away.

To do nothing is a choice and would reflect poor judgement on us all. This is not just my fight. It is one we need to make for future generations. I will now end my book like my husband used to end his e-mails with the Edmund Burke saying, "The only thing necessary for evil to triumph is for good men to do nothing."

Printed in the United States
By Bookmasters